HouseTransformed

HouseTransformed

Getting the Home You Want...

...with the House You Have

Matthew Schoenherr

WITH LINDA MASON HUNTER AND WENDY JORDAN

The Taunton Press

The Taunton Press
Inspiration for hands-on living®

The Taunton Press, Inc., 63 South Main Street,
PO Box 5506, Newtown, CT 06470-5506
e-mail: tp@taunton.com

Editor: Peter Chapman
Interior design: Debra McQuiston, Lori Wendin
Layout: Debra McQuiston, Lori Wendin
Illustrator: Christine Erikson

LIBRARY OF CONGRESS CATALOGING-IN-PUBLICATION DATA
Schoenherr, Matthew.
  House transformed : getting the home you want with the house you have /
Matthew Schoenherr,
Linda Hunter, Wendy Jordan ; photographs by Ken Gutmaker.
    p. cm.
  ISBN 1-56158-711-7
  1. Dwellings--Remodeling. 2. Architecture, Domestic--United States--
Designs and plans.
I. Hunter, Linda Mason. II. Jordan, Wendy Adler, 1946- III. Title.

  TH4816.S2826 2005
  690'.837--dc22
                                                        2004026818

Printed in the United States of America
10 9 8 7 6 5 4 3 2 1

The following manufacturers/names appearing in *House Transformed*
are trademarks: Corian®, Fireslate®, Plexiglas®

To the memory of
Michael Fuller, who transformed the
lives of everyone around him

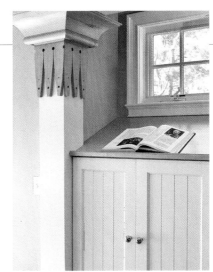

Acknowledgments

F irst, I wish to acknowledge the talent and contributions
of my co-authors Linda Hunter and Wendy Jordan whose
seasoned professionalism and dedication to the book were
so very welcome and whose team spirit was altogether inspiring.
Cheers to you both!

We three authors unanimously acknowledge the many talented
architects and wonderfully amenable homeowners whose projects
and transformed homes appear within the covers of this inspiring
book. Thank you all for your time and patience as we asked you
so many questions, only to follow up by invading your homes with
enough gear and equipment to film a major motion picture.

Our appreciation and respect go to publisher Jim Childs and the
many editors at The Taunton Press who had their hands full coordinating three authors, three photographers, sixteen architects, and
nineteen homeowners: thank you Maria Taylor, Peter Chapman,
Maureen Graney, Carolyn Mandarano, Paula Schlosser, Carol
Singer, Wendi Mijal, and the ever-special Robyn Doyon-Aitken. And
a warm thank you to AIA Knowledge Resources Director Richard
Hayes for his support of the Taunton mission.

The talents of photographers Rob Karosis, Ken Gutmaker, and
Chipper Hatter shine brightly on the pages that follow. A remarkable bunch of artists-on-the-go, these three gentlemen were faced
with demanding travel schedules, shadowing deadlines, and sometimes less-than-agreeable weather yet never failed to remain high-
spirited and prolific in capturing the hundreds of images required for
this book. Hats off to all.

Matthew Schoenherr, AIA

Contents

2   Introduction: Same House,
    Different Home

14   A Bigger, Better Bungalow

24   Transforming an Ugly Duckling

36   In Tune with Tradition

46   Style by Addition

56   A Craftsman Garage and Office

64   A Vermont Classic for Today

76   A Small, Multifunctional
     Add-On

82   Contemporary behind
     a Formal Façade

92   Colonial Transformation

100   Growing a Box on a Budget

112   From Cape to Bungalow

122   A-Frame Overhaul

132   Farmhouse Revised

142   Rescuing a Burned-Out Shell

152   Picture Perfect Porch

158   Cottage Fixer-Upper

168   Urban Townhouse Renewal

178   Design with a Difference

186   Architects and Designers

Same House, Different Home

as it was ...

Can a house shed its coat and emerge as something new? Can something as large as a house be transformed? Can one place become another? Yes. As stout and permanent as they may seem, houses are malleable—capable of change—proficient at flexing and shifting, stretching and growing, just like people.

Many of us live in houses we're not really happy with. The rooms are too small, the ceilings too low, the exterior lacks character, and the appliances, the fixtures, the tile, the hardware—you name it—are outdated, worn out, beyond repair. You've talked to your spouse, your friends, you've even called in carpenters and general contractors. "Replace the siding with maintenance-free vinyl," offers one. "It'll feel like a new home." "Tear it down and start over...it'll be easier than renovating," says another. You know that a new siding job won't solve your space limitations in the kitchen. And completely rebuilding your home, well, that seems overwhelming.

But what about another approach? What about *transforming* your home into something altogether new? OK, I can hear you say, that sounds like rebuilding. Well, that's partly true, but completely rebuilding is at one extreme end of the transformation spectrum. Through many years of practicing architecture and helping others

The original house (top photo) was in poor condition and lacked the space and jazzy outward appearance the homeowners wanted. Rather than flee to another neighborhood with larger homes, they adapted their home with an expressive addition that solves the problem of their architectural squeeze.

This new kitchen with fresh materials, clever storage solutions, and a practical layout is not in a new house. The bright new space is just one portion of a renewed home (shown at right) that has undergone a resourceful transformation.

Above, a dynamic new sitting space expands an upstairs room. Old space can be expanded too, as in the airy entry hall shown below where a ceiling was removed to gain light and height above the stair.

remodel their dark or cramped homes, I've found that just as there seems to be an endless amount of home types and styles, there are just as many ways to change these homes.

At the friendlier end of the spectrum, a successful transformation will involve the logical, practical adjustment of the floor plan: opening walls between rooms to create shared space, creating better walking paths through the house and eliminating "dead-end" spaces, or even finding new uses for rooms that are seldom used. Another level of house transformation involves rethinking how windows bring light into the interior of the home, and where exterior doors are positioned to allow uninhibited movement to the outdoors. But this is just the beginning. The character of your home can be transformed as well through the use of new materials and by thoughtfully creating exterior details that are expressive of the type of home you desire.

Working within Limits

A successful transformation might be as simple as an alteration of the floor plan. The only sign from the outside that something has changed at all might be the installation of a new window or two, or new doors leading to a terrace in the backyard. But on the interior, the changes to how the house lives, works, and feels can be dramatic: a kitchen closed off from other rooms in the house can be opened to the breakfast room beyond. A solid wall that separates this room from the family room is given an attractive new opening and suddenly it's easier to see, move, and share light between these busy areas of the house.

This example illustrates the basic architectural idea of open planning. Most older homes, and even many newer homes built using tired design concepts, are unnecessarily compartmentalized. The living areas of the home are divided into rooms that are too discreet for the type of casual lifestyle that many of us live today. It takes the *undoing* of these partitioned rooms—and the careful assigning of how the new, larger space is used—to gain new views throughout the home, increase the amount of natural light that travels deep into the interior, and create shared open areas for our common activities.

Onward and Outward

Your home might already be busting at the drywall seams. While altering interior partitions can create surprising spatial results and the feeling of a much enlarged house, the physical size of the home really hasn't changed. To successfully transform a home that's simply too small to begin with, you'll be faced with the larger project of adding on new square footage to accommodate the requirements of your growing family.

In many instances, a single addition that provides for a new kitchen and a family room will solve the need for more elbow room—this is the most commonly asked for project my architectural firm sees. In other cases, a new kitchen out the back or side may be combined with a new mudroom. At the front, expansion of the entry hall might be long overdue, while upstairs, there may be the need for

Opening rooms to one another helps a home to live larger through the creation of shared spaces. But there are other bonuses as well. Light from the outdoors can travel deeper into the interior of the home, and views through the home are extended.

This spirited kitchen addition departs from the usual rooms that are routinely tacked on to the back of a house. The curve of the ceiling is the most obvious departure and plays well against the straight-lined forms of the old house.

adding a new bedroom or the creation of a master bedroom suite made from a much smaller sleeping room. This involves the design of several additions positioned at different areas of the house. Now things have gotten more complicated—or in the case of a transformation, more advantageous, as this book will demonstrate.

Transforming the Entire House

The most ambitious project of all is a nearly complete reconstruction of your home, transforming it into something altogether new. I say *nearly complete* deliberately. For a transformation isn't merely knocking the house down and rebuilding completely new. A transformation involves a more resourceful and creative approach that reuses as much of the existing house as good design coupled with good luck will allow. The remodeling projects that have come through my office have all been constructed retaining major portions of the existing structure. We nearly always keep the foundation and the first floor structure, building the transformed home freshly

The owners of this gently remodeled home were careful to maintain a visual connection between the front and rear of the house to take advantage of natural light and draw visitors and family into the home.

atop the original—and valuable—base. Preferably, the inventive designer of the transformed house will also give careful consideration to holding onto the home's exterior walls—at least those that enclose the first floor.

The Blueprint for the Transformed Home

Because each house is as unique as its owner and the plot of land it sits on, no one book can tell you exactly how your home should be constructed or modified. Thankfully, there are some basic design guidelines that can help everyone from the first-timer to the veteran home renovator produce the best results possible. Whenever I embark on any new design project, I always refer to my own checklist of seven essential items that should never be overlooked (I call them the "7 Knows"). These elements of designing the transformed home that every homeowner should know are listed on the next two pages.

as it was ...

A house transformation doesn't mean knocking down the original and starting over. Though the size of this California home and the architectural style have changed dramatically, glimpses of the older home's profile remain.

The 7 Essentials of Remodeling

1. Know Your Place

Acknowledge your region, town, or city

There's an importance to understanding the established fabric of a region that is often taken for granted. Recognizing and respecting the distinct character of your community and incorporating local patterns of building into your new design strengthens the framework of the regional context and contributes to the overall sense of a unique place.

2. Know Your Property

Respond to your site

The transformation of your home will be most successful when the design responds to the favorable features and climate conditions of your site—and addresses the negative factors as well by blocking an unwanted view or creating a barrier for privacy.

3. Know Your House

Understand how to design compatibly

This doesn't mean simply matching the design of new construction with old. To truly transform a house—and to do it with distinction—you must logically combine new and old planning patterns, forms, and infrastructure.

4. Know Your Structure

Understand how to design safely

Design your home or addition so that it conforms to the requirements of the building code enforced in your region. Explore structural solutions, whether they are daring or reserved, to the point that doesn't exceed the capabilities of your construction team.

5. Know Your Palette

Select materials that withstand the test of time

The construction materials that protect our families from frosty winters and boiling summers have to perform agreeably in their respective tasks. Additionally, textures, patterns, and colors of roofing, siding, cabinets, and floors express an architectural identity that can become a visual clamor unless selected with care.

6. Know Your Lifestyle

Work to create a design that supports the way you live

Family activities and rituals have their own particular spatial needs: public rooms for gathering and entertaining, a quiet place for reading, and private areas for guests, working at home, and sleeping.

7. Know Your Passions

Design to evoke emotion

Be honest about your own desires and incorporate the things into your home that matter the most and reward the senses. It's OK to give your home, and yourself, a couple of extra feet in a hallway, or to get rid of an attic space and create a tall ceiling—all for sheer drama or whimsy. Make your home your own and try not to think too much about resale or what the neighbors are doing.

as it was ...

The remodeled home shown above was fully renovated atop its former foundation. The exterior walls and the central single-story roof are from the original.

A House Transformed

How can this abstract group of guidelines be applied to something as tangible as a house? The choice of walls, windows, and materials that make up a transformed house will be the direct result of a thorough understanding of all the 7 Essentials of Remodeling. As an example, let's look at the following remodeled home that my firm recently worked on.

A couple with three small children approached us to design their dream home. But this was not a new house to be built from the foundation up. They had purchased a pastoral 2-acre parcel in an outlying area of Westport, Connecticut, with an unattractive low-slung, ranch-style house sitting square in the middle.

The character of Stan and Helene's new house needed to be completely reinvented—transformed. Though ranch homes stand solidly on their own merit, the couple chose their homesite for the property flush with flowing lawns and mature trees. They didn't choose a house while shopping for a new home—they chose the place for their family to live and grow. First things first—you needed to **know your place** and acknowledge the region and town. Designing successfully for Stan and Helene meant understanding the greater region where this house called home. To define the region, we first look at the neighborhood and take stock of the house types. Second, we study the rural area of town that contains the outlying neighborhoods. Next, the character of the town itself gives us certain design clues, as does the architecture of Connecticut and the greater region of New England.

We proposed that the family's new home have the character of a classic farmhouse—a type of house that would make a good fit in the neighborhood. This would mean adding a second floor to create the characteristic high gable roofs of a farmhouse. A common attribute of a classic farmhouse is a covered front porch extending across the front facade. Which brings us to the second guideline: **know your property** and respond to your site. The porch reinforced the type of architecture we were to propose, and the position of the house on the property made the porch a logical choice.

The third crucial transformation guideline is **know your house** and understand how to design compatibly. We chose to reuse the entire footprint of the former ranch. And one significant space in the old house shaped the appearance of our finished farmhouse—a large, open living room that links the twin gables of the new second floor. A tall ceiling in the center of the home created an unavoidable separation between the left half of the home and the right when we proposed to add a second floor for bedrooms. The solution was to construct two second floors, each with their own staircase on either side of the vaulted space.

Fourth, and very important: **know your structure** and understand how to design safely. The success of the open central living room meant the removal of some obtrusive ceiling beams which cut the effect of the room's height. But these beams acted as ties, guarding against the lateral thrust of the sloping roof. If removed, another method of supporting the structure would have to be devised. We chose to support the roof with long-span steel beams positioned further up the ceiling line. The new supports are better integrated

Spaces unfold along this view through the heart of the home in a design technique known as layering. The layered spaces are open to one another—from the family room, through the kitchen, and into the dining area beyond—yet retain an identity of their own.

The original stone fireplace was visually overwhelming for the renovated space. The dark stone was covered instead with a lighter-toned overmantel of varnished maple.

with the surface of the ceiling and allow the ceiling to soar skyward seemingly unrestrained.

The fifth essential item is **know your palette**. The details of the house would bring the New England character to life—clapboard siding, painted, built-up wood trim at the windows, doors, rakes and fascias, painted wood posts with additive details appropriate for the style, and wood double-hung windows with authentic divided lights.

The sixth essential guideline is to **know your lifestyle**. The area the family considers to be the true heart of the home is the kitchen. Stan and Helene's kitchen is a comfortable, functional work area, flanked on one side by the everyday eating area and on the other by a generous family room where parents and kids can flop down informally with a drink in one hand and the television remote in the other. A passageway through the kitchen connects the spaces by foot, while low walls connect the spaces by sight. It's essentially one

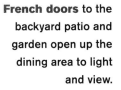

French doors to the backyard patio and garden open up the dining area to light and view.

The spirit of a classic Connecticut farmhouse came from the shell of a former 1960s ranch. An attribute that reinforces the style is the covered porch that stretches across the entire front facade. Details and materials common to the area, such as native stone, wood clapboard siding, and painted woodwork, further anchor the home to the greater region.

big comfortable space where the family spends more time than anywhere else in the house.

To successfully transform your home you must provide for the seventh and final guideline: **know your passions** and design to evoke emotion. In the end, the owners moved forward to achieve the results for their living needs, and moved back—through time—for the answers and inspiration to create a home in the style they appreciated.

Stan and Helene were able to complete their project more quickly and with fewer compromises by recognizing the hidden value in their overlooked foundation and the old walls. By thinking resourcefully and building atop what at first seemed to be a throw-away home, they were able to reduce their construction expenses and realize their dreams for a home that works for their lifestyle and displays a refreshed outward appearance.

Let's take a look now at how a number of other homeowners across America have worked with today's top architects and designers to entirely redefine what once seemed so unchangeable.

Inside the house, details on the newel post and stairway trim echo the columns of the front porch.

A Bigger, Better Bungalow

Make the style consistent throughout the house

Bring in more light

Create an inviting family room

Add a master bedroom suite

Give the family space to spread out

Capture views of the back and side yards

Some houses make a great first impression; you need to live in them for a while to let the truth come out. Take this 1916 bungalow in Washington, D.C. The homeowners had stars in their eyes when they found the charming house in a verdant old neighborhood. Not only was it a bungalow, a style they loved, but they needed a family room and this house had a big one that had been added in the 1980s. They snapped up the house and moved in, certain that they and their two children would enjoy many happy hours together in the family room.

Well, that never happened. The bulk of the 400-sq.-ft. family room was several steps down from the main house and jutted off awkwardly to the side. The room was isolated, gloomy, and cavernous. It ate up most of the backyard. And its roof leaked. The family rarely used the room; in fact, after contending with the persistent leak, they started to hate it.

as it is today

The deep roof overhang shields the family room from the sun and provides rain shelter for the deck. The balcony, over the deck door, offers extra weather protection.

The kitchen flows into both the breakfast area and the seating cluster in the new space. A bank of large windows and a glass door open the space to the walkout deck.

Dark woodwork made the rest of the house look somber and dated. The second floor, an old addition, was a cramped warren, and the basement was unusable because the ceilings were too low. Architect Ralph Cunningham of Cunningham + Quill Architects in Washington, D.C., replaced the hulking family room with a better-positioned two-story addition that contains a 250-sq.-ft. family room/breakfast area, a large deck, and a second-floor master suite with balcony. He also spiffed up the original house with repairs and light finishes and excavated the basement.

Cleaning Up the Floor Plan

The new plan is a study in simplicity and symmetry. In contrast to the squirrelly 1980s add-on, the new one is a clean, rectangular room on the same floor level as the other living spaces. The smaller

The scale and character of the existing parlor and dining room helped set the tone for the new space. Flooring, trim, windows, slim dividing walls, and even the dining room bay window are echoed in the addition.

rectangle of the adjacent kitchen melds with the breakfast area across a wide opening. The new room is centered along the back of the house, just as a large, rectangular deck is centered along the back of the room itself. A glass door, between large paired windows in the center of the family room wall, leads out to the deck. Open yet ordered, accessible yet gracious, the new room is a pleasure to use.

To soften and embellish the simple geometry, Cunningham sprinkled the addition with more complex, ornamental elements modeled after the original bungalow. Bay windows on each side of the family room repeat the graceful arc of the dining room bay. The new molding, window casing, and double-hung windows—with 16 lights above and single sash below—match the old. Simple but handsome wood cabinetry and open shelving reinforce the house's clean-cut,

Partially recessed, the master bedroom cabinet accommodates deep drawers and shelves without absorbing much floor space. It matches the other cabinetry in the house.

The pitched roof of the addition tees into the main roof, breaking the bungalow into sections so it doesn't look uncharacteristically bulky. Shed dormers yield extra space for the master bath and bed alcove.

The exterior trim is simply detailed and meticulously ordered for a classic American look that harmonizes with the original house.

all-American character. On the exterior, deep eaves with exposed rafters echo those on the original bungalow. Artful touches, such as the delicate balcony guardrail and the fancy cut ends on the rafters, display classic Craftsman attention to detail.

Shaping a Versatile Space

The new family room is smaller than the old one in square footage but bigger and more versatile in function. The bay windows make the difference. Popping out of the sides of the room, they facilitate two furniture groupings. The bay closest to the kitchen outlines a sunny niche for a breakfast table. Fitted with a wraparound bench, the bay at the other end anchors a cluster of comfortable chairs where family and friends can flop down to chat. This bay can also be enjoyed as a tranquil little retreat. But slide in a table, and the homeowners can use it as an extra seating place for the Thanksgiving dinner crowd.

Know Your Lifestyle

THE HOMEOWNERS PREFER to enjoy the backyard without being in it. They are not gardeners and like to savor the lush greenery from a comfortable distance. A raised deck makes perfect sense for them because it is surrounded by grass and trees but separated from the bugs and dirt.

With two teenagers, the family needs both "together" space and getaway space. The open family room/kitchen area works well as the together place, where the kids can grab a snack, do homework, watch TV, and talk with their parents. When their friends come over, the teens head down to the basement. The homeowners can get away, too. In addition to their master bedroom suite, each has a study—one on the main floor and the other in a spare bedroom upstairs.

Bay windows on each side of the family room capture light and panoramic views of the landscaped side yards. This one, with built-in bench seating, is a cozy nook but wide enough for a table so that it can provide extra seating for parties or holidays.

A fraternal twin to the bay window at the other end of the addition, the bay on the kitchen end is more casual. This one gives shape to a sunny breakfast area.

Where New Meets Old

The seam between the existing house and the addition is invisible, which is exactly what the homeowners wanted. Wood flooring runs continuously from the original kitchen into the new room, and the classic cabinetry and molding match perfectly throughout. Further binding the spaces, the kitchen island laps over the line into the family room. To give the new room a suggestion of place, though, Cunningham traced the perimeter with ceiling trim tied to the exposed beam.

From the street, you might never notice that the house had an addition. Roofing, siding, trim bands, window trim, and color are all the same. The windows are the same style, the proportion of window to wall is the same, the deep eaves match, and both old and new roof sections have exposed rafters. The addition streams off the back of the house, connecting so smoothly that it looks as if it has always been there.

Rooflines, windows, bays, and trim align along the side of the house, uniting old and new.

That's not all these window bays do. The family room is a little narrower than the existing house so as not to overwhelm the structure; from the street it is barely visible. Only the bay windows stretch out to the bungalow's side boundaries. They extend like shallow prows into the side yards, filling the room with filtered light and peaceful views. In other words, they absorb less of the yard than a full-width addition would and enable the homeowners to enjoy it more.

Great Moves

Cunningham used the surprise factor to give the lofty master bedroom some extra punch. Originally, the upstairs hall ended in a narrow stub. When he extended the hallway to the new bedroom, Cunningham kept it narrow. As you approach the room, you walk through a tight passageway with closet doors on each side. Then, at the bedroom entry, the space bursts open with high ceilings, a shower of sunlight, and long, verdant views.

before and after

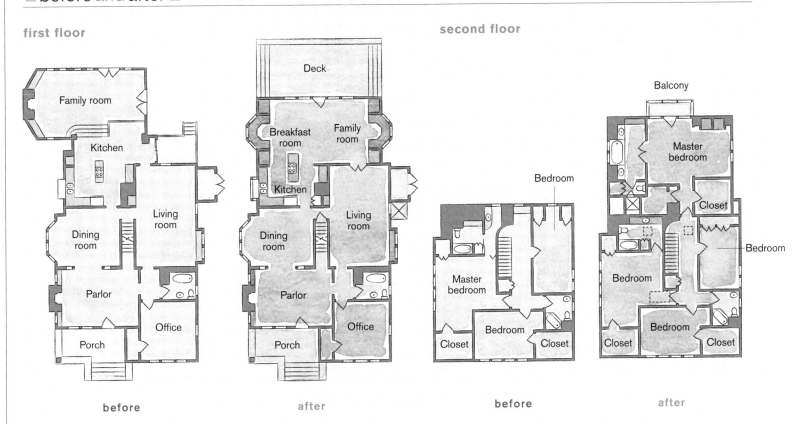

first floor

before

after

second floor

before

after

A slim wall and ceiling trim subtly separate the sleeping alcove from the master bedroom's sunny sitting area, with its balcony and large windows. This gentle boundary makes the open space feel like a suite of rooms.

Fine ornamental details form a pleasing counterpoint to the clean rectangles and ordered placement of rooms in the addition. The palette of molding profiles and color bands, shown here in the master bedroom, takes its cue from existing rooms and is applied throughout the house.

Sweet Master Suite

The master suite is like a present in a gift box. On the outside it looks simple enough—a rectangular box over the family room, with shed dormers on each side. Under that unassuming wrap is a serene getaway with lots of deluxe features.

From the narrow upstairs hall, the suite remains "under wraps." At the threshold of the suite, the excitement unfolds. Walking in, you suddenly find yourself in a spacious, light-filled sitting area. Ahead is a span of glass overlooking the balcony and surrounding views. Above is an expansive tray ceiling. The room's ambiance is light and luxurious.

Like the family room below it, the master suite is a cleanly organized open space. A band high on the walls dramatizes the high ceiling but also forms a consistent base line around the room. It connects smoothly to a beam marking the entry point to the tranquil sleeping alcove. His and hers walk-in closets make good use of windowless interior space adjacent to the bedroom.

One of the shed dormers creates headroom and window space for the sleeping alcove. The other, directly opposite, carves out an alcove for the whirlpool tub in the master bathroom. Two sinks fit into wall niches on each side of the tub, leaving a clean rectangle of

floor area. Almost 18 ft. long, the classy bathroom has ample space for a built-in dressing table and a shower/commode compartment. Mirrors cover structural walls, melting them away visually and washing the room with reflected light. With its double doors open, the bathroom is an appealing picture that enhances the bedroom.

The balcony, wrapped in a pretty Chippendale rail, is another visual treat (see the photo on p. 21). In fact, it's a whole bundle of good things. It's a place to sip tea in the morning, to read the paper, to sit and enjoy the sun and fresh air. Door flung open, it extends the suite to the outdoors. A little luxury like this balcony, only 3 ft. by 10 ft., is an indulgence most homeowners can afford. As the saying goes, nice things come in small packages.

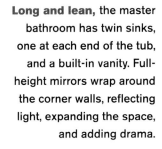

Long and lean, the master bathroom has twin sinks, one at each end of the tub, and a built-in vanity. Full-height mirrors wrap around the corner walls, reflecting light, expanding the space, and adding drama.

The entry to the master bath is gracious and spacious. Double doors frame an elegant view of the whirlpool tub and paired windows that line up with matching windows at the other end of the bedroom.

Transforming
An Ugly Duckling

When Todd Chessher found this 60-year-old laborer's cottage, the years had not been kind to it. A series of poorly done remodelings had robbed the house of its personality, and, the final indignity, vinyl siding covered up all street-facing windows, leaving the house without a "face." Inside, the house was lifeless—with everything painted white, few windows, and dirty off-white carpet or faux parquet linoleum covering the floor.

A real estate prowler by nature and profession, Todd is always on the lookout for a forlorn house with good bones in an up-and-coming neighborhood. When he found this ugly duckling on a quiet street in Tarrytown, Tex. (just north of downtown Austin), he knew it had potential. It would take an architect with vision to do the job right.

Built in the 1940s, this small Austin house has always been a modest frame cottage. A total top-to-bottom renovation reinforces that aesthetic, letting the house be what it wants to be while staying within budget guidelines.

Where New Meets Old

The only addition in this 1,800-sq.-ft. renovation occurred at the front entry, where 30 sq. ft. of the former porch was recaptured as interior space and converted into a spare vestibule open to the living room. Bright red paint covers the walls of this little space, creating a warm welcome. Glass in the front door permits a direct view into the new area.

Dining and living areas share a single large space. A more intimate ante-room (defined on one corner by the orange column) acts as the gateway to the bedroom wing and signals that this is a quiet part of the home.

Architect David Webber saw the possibilities: Remove vinyl siding, uncover hidden windows, add lots more windows, rework the front entry, and the house could be a charmer. Other than the obvious aesthetic flaws, the house was in great shape—with hardwood floors underneath linoleum, decent wood trim, and good existing doors. The price was right and the location superb—a quaint tree-lined neighborhood of one- and two-story houses built between the 1930s and late 1950s.

With a limited budget, economy became priority number one: how to get the most efficient use of space, finished with quality materials, without spending a lot of money.

Rethinking the Floor Plan

Over the years the flow of the house had been lost, resulting in a clunky floor plan of tiny rooms with an internal hallway that made

Great Moves

Before the remodel, this cottage had a crooked spine, the result of several poorly planned earlier remodelings. Architect David Webber straightened the center hall and opened the kitchen to the back den, where there's a good connection with the outdoors through a wall of French doors leading to a new deck.

The original 8-ft. by 10-ft. back bedroom (now a study) was extended into the den 4 ft., creating one continuous wall running almost full length through the middle of the house, front to back. This is the most interesting wall of the house with three special features built into it: a corner bench alcove off the kitchen (the hub of the house), a 5-ft. by 9-ft. anteroom (used as an art gallery) supported by a single column in the living room, and an entry alcove (with much-needed coat closet).

before and after

first floor

before

after

Light from the big front window in the master bath spills over into the bedroom, giving a sense of larger space. Double doors separating the two rooms contain frosted glass, providing a degree of privacy while still allowing soft diffuse light into the bedroom. Two doors centered in the room lend an element of grandeur—a big gesture for a modest home.

In lieu of a medicine cabinet, a low sidewall in the master bath is built out 5 in., creating cabinet storage with a shelf on top, a smart space-saving solution.

Formerly an oversized closet carved out of the original front porch, the master bath looks onto the street through a large divided window that mimics the one in the living room. A privacy blind pulls up to cover the lower two-thirds of the window, keeping the upper third open for light and fresh air. The tongue-and-groove ceiling is original.

THE SEVEN

Know Your House

EVEN WITH THE REMUDDLINGS, this was always a modest frame cottage, plain and simple. Since the budget was limited, architect David Webber decided not to fight the basic nature of the house. Let it be what it wants to be, became the mantra, just make it a better version of itself.

In keeping with this philosophy, original hardwood flooring (in good shape throughout the house) was left intact, even though the type of wood differed from one area to the next. Pulling out perfectly good materials in order to get a match doesn't fit the concept of cottage simplicity. Continuous flooring helps with the scale of the house, too. Changing flooring materials from area to area appears chaotic, making a small house feel even smaller. Organizing the interior by color is another small-scale trick that enlivens the house inexpensively without changing trim, doors, or anything else that was basically okay.

Architectural details help reinforce the cottage aesthetic. Accent windows are a nice cottage touch, as is the little flat-roofed awning over the front porch, V-groove kitchen cabinets, painted wood paneling in the den, and bathroom wainscoting. An eclectic mixture of traditional and modern furniture contributes to the ambience.

you feel stuck walking around in circles. The kitchen was outdated and cheaply finished; the entire back of the house was dark and poorly planned. The master bedroom, with its ugly entry and over-large closet, needed a total renovation. Webber cleverly reworked the floor plan, losing little to hallways yet giving each quiet area the privacy it needed. Rearranging walls and changing the location of doorways transformed a two-bedroom/two-bath plan into one with three bedroom suites (one doubles as a study), each with its own bath. The entrance of the master bedroom was relocated so it faces its own little hallway, with a closet on either side of the entry. Air-conditioning and the water heater were moved to the attic, making room for a washer/dryer right outside the master suite. The large master closet/dressing room (an early remodeling carved from the original front porch) became a spacious master bath with a wall of windows that floods the master suite with light all day long.

Painting the window muntins deep plum adds depth, guiding the eye to the interior rather than stopping it abruptly at the window.

A generous grouping of windows in the renovated living room floods the interior with sunlight and neighborhood views. The small windows at top act as transoms placed high on the wall.

But by far the biggest architectural intervention came from moving a couple of walls to open up living spaces to views and light. From the street side, you can see clear through the house out the back door, making the house feel larger than its 1,800 sq. ft. Several special places keep the open plan from feeling cavernous, including a sunny kitchen gathering spot, a spotlit art gallery, and an inviting private entry.

Giving the House a Face

In one bold stroke, the dysfunctional, introverted personality of this house was completely transformed. Where the front façade was windowless, now two generous window groups reside at each side of the front entry, giving the house a face again.

The living room opening is the larger of the two—one 5-ft.-wide by 3½-ft.-high fixed picture window flanked by tall casement windows, all with divided lights. This grouping is topped by a bank of much smaller square windows positioned as though they were transsoms. The effect is extremely dramatic on the interior, where the window-over-window grouping makes the ceiling appear taller. Because we're used to seeing transom windows high overhead in a room, the lower-positioned transoms, fitting beneath conventional ceiling height, tricks us into believing the room is much taller.

On the exterior, the square windows become vital components within a wide painted band that encircles the house like a huge ribbon, arranging the façade into an orderly composition. In addition to cleverly containing the gang of small windows and adding horizontal emphasis, the banding creates welcome vertical stacking as well, providing emphasis beneath the thin fascia and lending a strong, baselike appearance where the roof springs from the cottage walls.

Newly installed French doors provide welcome access from the den to a new backyard deck. Cooks in the centrally positioned kitchen can now enjoy outdoor views while benefiting from nearby natural light.

A new deck across the back of the house becomes an outdoor room when the weather is cooperative. French doors lead to the den and nearby kitchen.

as it was ...

31

The entry, with its rich vermillion walls, creates a spare and easy welcome to the adjacent living room, which is painted in calming shades of gray. Flooring (once part of the front porch) is scored concrete.

Organizing with Color

Even after renovation, the house remains a typical cottage, its rooms laid out with no apparent overriding order. The least expensive way to give such an interior a sense of organization (as well as delight) is with color. Consequently, each suite of rooms and adjoining hallway uses one family of colors linked by a common trim color.

There are 39 interior colors in all, creating a fun, moody house that offers a different experience from one space to the next. The master bedroom suite, for example, is painted in mustard-lemon gray hues. The kitchen and den are shades of blue with a splash of limey citrus. The entry vestibule is rich vermillion. Living and dining

Small Moves

Cabinets for a Small Kitchen

In lieu of conventional kitchen cabinets, this transformed Texas kitchen uses open shelving that provides instant accessibility for dishware and glasses. Storing even your everyday items out in the open can create an attractive display of texture and color, similar to a bookcase in a library. Since every inch counts in a small house, the absence of cabinet doors adds depth, creating an illusion of more space.

These slab-like shelves (made from 1½-in.-thick fiberboard) project from the wall with the aid of a hidden steel angle mounted to the wall. Slender supports at the front of the shelf (made from inexpensive steel bar-stock) hang from the ceiling without hindering storage space. Exposed steel supports coated with a clear lacquer to prevent oxidation are a nice complement to the owner's commercial-style appliances.

Though not enlarged, the kitchen was entirely gutted and reworked for efficiency. It now shares a half-wall with the den that's both a separator and a snack counter. Access to a comfy benched nook (the hub of the house) is gained through the archway. V-groove cabinets lend a cottage-style touch, while the counter-top and backsplash are local limestone tile.

Like the adjacent living area, the dining room is painted in shades of gray, a palette that unites the two rooms into one big open space. The wall at right runs almost completely through the middle of the house, separating public from private spaces. The doorway peeks through the kitchen, into the den and beyond to the rear deck and backyard.

rooms are fields of soothing, warm grays. The middle hallway is painted deep lilac and eggplant, and the study walls are various shades of green. Color jazzes up the exterior, too, where five natural colors blend beautifully with the trees and landscaping.

Cheerful livability is the reward reaped from this top-to-bottom remodeling. Other than the roof (which was new) and foundation work, the entire house was renovated, all appliances and utilities replaced, including plumbing and air conditioning. What was once a dreary, depressing house nobody wanted is now a thoroughly modern, light-filled jewel, an authentic slice of Americana, Texas style.

as it was …

Windows placed high on the den's sidewall provide both natural light and privacy from nearby neighbors, allowing the focus to center on the French doors and rear deck. High windows also accomplish an architectural purpose, creating an illusion of taller space.

In Tune
with Tradition

WISH LIST

Bring back the house's
Colonial character

Create a family-friendly
interior

Take advantage of outdoor
views

Emphasize outdoor access

Move the master bedroom
suite to the front of the
house

Home improvement does not necessarily mean modernization. In fact, for a house with a historical pedigree, the best remodeling approach may be a return to tradition rather than an infusion of trendy updates. When Doug and Lisa Tanner bought their 1920 Colonial Revival foursquare in Minneapolis, they couldn't wait to erase all the ill-conceived modernizations that had been inflicted on it and bring back its dignified Colonial character.

Doug, a remodeling contractor, discovered the house when meeting with neighbors about a remodeling project. The location was dreamy—a row of solid, old houses on a small, quiet street that's in the heart of the city yet directly across from a lagoon and extensive, wooded parkland. When he saw the "for sale" sign out front, Doug was captivated: What a place for a family that enjoys the rustic outdoors as much as the attractions of urban living.

Now at the front of the house where formal rooms belong in traditional Colonial designs, the dining room enhances the gracious entry. The stair newels and balusters reflect Colonial patterns, as does the trim framing the dining room entryway.

The house had been updated repeatedly over the years, losing much of its Colonial integrity. The worst indignity was recent: a 1990s flat-topped, two-story rear addition that nearly doubled the house's size but was a stylistic misfit. With that addition, the house had plenty of space—4,230 sq. ft.—but it was poorly arranged and, despite its size, seemed cramped. Doug and Lisa asked Rehkamp Larson Architects to revamp the floor plan to make a comfortable home for their family of four and to take full advantage of parkland views. Mark Larson and Susan Nackers Ludwig of Rehkamp Larson added just 600 sq. ft. but created a spacious house that is both a stately Colonial and a bright, view-oriented, family-friendly residence. Doug's firm, Dovetail Renovation, did the construction.

The screened sun porch mixes the solidity of a room with the breeziness of the outdoors. Doug used Tennessee flagstone for the flooring and inset a sleek steel cabinet to keep firewood handy.

Small Moves

Porch Fireplace

Adding a fireplace to the screen porch gave the Tanners an outdoor room that can be used year-round, even in Minnesota's climate. On brisk evenings in the spring and fall, the fireplace warms the room enough for a cozy dinner al fresco. In winter, after skating on the lagoon across the street, the family can huddle around the fireplace and drink hot chocolate. The big, brick fireplace is hardy but handsome, just right for a room that is used as both an outdoor area and an extension of the polished living space.

Classic Spaces, Contemporary Comforts

In a traditional Colonial, the formal, public rooms are showcased in front and the more casual, private spaces cluster in back. Doug and Lisa's house had it almost backwards, with the family room by the front door and the dining room in back. Rehkamp Larson flip-flopped those rooms so that the elegant dining room and living room now straddle the center hall in the traditional manner. At the back of the house is the family center—a sunny family room that flows freely into the kitchen, the mudroom, and the backyard patio.

A flimsy screened enclosure squandered the prime location at the front corner of the house. Rehkamp Larson replaced it with a more substantial sun porch that is handsome enough to be an extension of the formal entertainment area yet irresistible as a family hangout and casual outdoor room.

Doug and Lisa, both avid cooks, also like to spend time in the kitchen. That's why Rehkamp Larson enlarged the kitchen, adding more counters and a big island. A broad opening to the family room

The family room window bay adds sunlight, seating, and storage without absorbing floor area. Inset cabinetry provides display space and a television niche without intruding on the room's tidy, traditional styling.

as it was ...

Great Moves

Service spaces such as bathrooms, closets, and mudrooms belong where they won't be in the way. The existing mudroom and powder room cut into the adjacent kitchen and dining room, cramping circulation and essentially shrinking those rooms. Rehkamp Larson took them out, releasing floor area for a spacious, well-connected kitchen-family room area.

The new mudroom and powder room are bigger and better, too. Rehkamp Larson clustered them at the back corner of the house, where the powder room still is convenient to the living area and gathers light from high windows to the sun porch.

The mudroom has plenty of space for a bench and a big closet lined with drawers and shelves. The mudroom door is directly across the yard from the garage door.

■ before and after ■

first floor

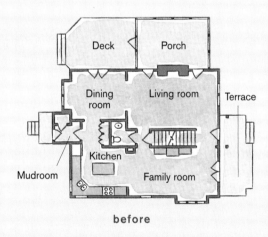

before

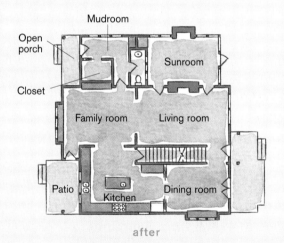

after

second floor

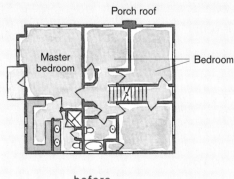

before

after

lets them keep an eye on their two young children and watch the evening news on television. Instead of cutting into the kitchen space to make a breakfast nook, the Tanners decided to restore the time-honored practice of eating all family meals in the dining room. The wide doorway between the kitchen and dining room stays open most of the time, but it can be closed with pocket doors to hide kitchen clutter when dinner guests come.

The upstairs plan was backwards in another respect: The master bedroom suite, part of the 1990s rear addition, was in exactly the wrong place to enjoy views of the lagoon. Rehkamp Larson not only moved the master bedroom front and center to command the best scenery but also added a private sitting room and a spacious master

Raised-panel wainscoting, an antique reproduction chandelier, and a vintage sideboard give the dining room a true Colonial look, and the wallpaper conforms to 1920s Colonial Revival tradition. French doors open the room to the terrace and scenic vistas.

The luxurious marble flooring and countertop, claw-foot tub, and lustrous wainscoting in the master bath recall the 1920 Colonial Revival era. Since the room is over the sun porch, Doug used well-insulated radiant-floor heating to keep the pipes from freezing.

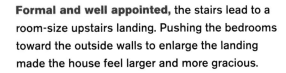

Formal and well appointed, the stairs lead to a room-size upstairs landing. Pushing the bedrooms toward the outside walls to enlarge the landing made the house feel larger and more gracious.

bathroom in the sunny corner over the sun porch. A large master closet occupies interior space.

Doug and Lisa wanted the upstairs to be as gracious and spacious as the main floor, but it felt cramped, with all four bedrooms and the kids' bath crowded around a skimpy landing. Larson reoriented rooms and pushed them to the outside walls to free space for a 12-ft. by 11-ft. landing that is airy, welcoming, and big enough for a comfortable chair or two.

Special Rooms for Family Living

The house was gutted for the remodel, but it acquired a fine patina nevertheless. That's because Doug applied Colonial-style finishes in almost every

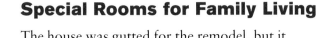

Doug applied the same Colonial-style crown molding and window frames throughout the house. The high windows in this child's bedroom match those in the laundry room for a symmetrical look from the outside.

room—richly stained plank flooring; painted wood cabinetry; molding, newels, and balusters in traditional profiles; even the mortised door hardware. With such quality and consistency, the house rings true as a Colonial Revival structure.

But even in a traditional house, there is room for some indulgences. Doug and Lisa's house sparkles with nuggets of space that have been custom-tailored to suit the family's lifestyle. On the main floor, they have the sun porch, where the family congregates all the time, and the big, practical mudroom. An upstairs gem is the sitting room, a snug, sun-drenched getaway that Doug and Lisa call their treehouse because its lagoon view is framed by sweeping pine branches.

Another upstairs pleasure, surprisingly enough, is the laundry room. It's convenient to the bedrooms, where most of the laundry goes; it's big, at 14 ft. by 9 ft.; and it has everything, from pullout

The cozy sitting room in the master suite occupies a prime corner at the front of the house, overlooking the lagoon and park. Doug and Lisa use it as a quiet retreat for reading or working on a laptop.

Doug removed the limestone surround on the living room fireplace, replaced it with classic brick, and installed a Colonial-style, painted wood mantel. French doors alongside the fireplace open the room to the sun porch and to fresh air.

Because it is visible from the upstairs landing, the laundry room had to be attractive. It shares the classic cabinetry, moldings, plank flooring, gleaming windows, and clean, white finish of the rest of the house; cabinet doors hide the machines and laundry.

A tall cabinet holds the stacked, full-size washing machine and dryer. Clothes are sorted into four glide-out bins.

sorting hampers to a drying area, a counter for folding, a utility sink, and a large, shelf-lined closet. As the first room you see at the top of the stairs, it's also high profile. A clean-cut space wrapped in white-painted cabinetry and filled with light from generous windows, it exudes a classic beauty that does the house proud.

Keeping Traditions on the Exterior

One key ingredient of the Colonial style is symmetry, and Rehkamp Larson Architects were careful to respect that characteristic on the front of the house. The front door remains central, surrounded by symmetrically arranged windows and similarly scaled patio doors. The side addition steps back from the main structure so it neither throws off the symmetry nor makes the house look too massive. Narrow lap siding is a Colonial classic, as are the soft gray color, white trim, and simple rails that dress up the entry portico and terrace. Although taller than standard to capture extra sun and views, all of the doors and windows are divided-light units with small panes.

In back, Rehkamp Larson could relax the Colonial rules a bit. Here they combined symmetry with the added-onto look of Colonial houses that accumulated annexes through the years. The middle section extends into the yard, which emphasizes the importance of this central element and boosts space in the family room and the bedroom above it. The classic, gable roof of this central section matches the roof of the main house and links neatly to it. As for the wide central bay, it is there as much to soften the back of the house with shape and shadow lines as to provide a window seat in the family room.

There is a note of appealing randomness in the back of the house. On one side of the gabled section is the mudroom entry. The little entry landing with its sheltering roof is a friendly, useful extension to the outdoors. On the other side is a cedar deck that opens to the family room. A Colonial deck? George Washington may not have had one, but this deck, squared off and painted to match, is as Colonial as it can be.

The gabled section does such a good job of centering the rear exterior that the imperfect symmetry and the flat roofs of the side sections don't matter.

THE SEVEN

Know Your Place

THE TANNERS' 1920 Colonial Revival house occupies a place in history as well as a place in a picturesque part of the city. Doug and Lisa wanted the design to reflect both. With its clapboard-look cement fiber siding, traditional trim, and strong symmetry, the façade has a classic character that acknowledges its Colonial heritage and harmonizes with the other early-1900s houses on the block.

Even so, the house basks in its proximity to the lagoon and parkland across the street. All the new window and door openings are a few inches taller than the old ones to capitalize on the scenic vista. The porch and upstairs sitting area occupy the front of the wing on the side of the house, where they can absorb the woodsy ambiance, too. The wing is set back 2½ ft., though, and sheltered behind a grand, old pine tree where it doesn't compromise the scale and symmetry of the traditional Colonial façade.

Style By Addition

WISH LIST

Provide more communal living space downstairs

Expand the office/guest room

Relocate the washer/dryer upstairs

Create a meditation perch

Add space in the son's bedroom

This reinvented house defines a whole new style, what its owner, Mindy Green, likes to call "beachy modern." It is located in a southern Connecticut town, once a seashore community of rental houses and beach shacks, but now a prosperous little pocket on Long Island Sound where small rental units have morphed into glorious beach homes, houses as big as you can grow them on postage-stamp lots.

Chuck and Mindy Green invested in the community in the early 1980s, purchasing a one-story uninsulated summer house, a dowdy 1,000-sq.-ft. red-painted ranch encircled by a chain-link fence on a tiny 6,000-sq.-ft. lot. They soon added an 800-sq.-ft. second story to accommodate the needs of a family, but they didn't have much of a budget. When their children became teenagers, the couple decided to transform the house into something fresh and modern, relieving it of darkness and congestion and opening up small rooms for space and light.

as it is today

A low-shingled overhang creates a sheltered, welcoming entrance. The tapered metal column supports the roof and adds architectural interest.

Where New Meets Old

On the exterior, it's clear what is old and what is new. All wood-shingled parts are new additions, as are wide clapboard sections without corner boards, painted light gray. Existing pieces retain their original narrow clapboard siding with corner boards and are painted a darker gray. Although they differ in form and material, old and new are cohesively bound by smart composition and a few shared details, such as window trim and rake and eaves details. Inside, old and new blend seamlessly into one complete whole.

In the great room, subtle clues define functions. Wood columns where a wall used to be separate the dining and living rooms, and a change in floor level defines the kitchen from the dining room. The kitchen island straddles the step with a curvy overhang to contrast with the geometric lines of the house.

Strict setback requirements and footprint restrictions limited the size and placement of expansions, making the design a real challenge. After nine months of rejected ideas, architect Michael Stein (of Stein/Troost Architecture) came up with a design that completely invigorates the floor plan, bringing down walls and opening up the main living space so the heart of the home can live fuller and brighter.

A Story of Little Additions

Given a limited budget, the architect's approach was to expand the house with two two-story additions and a few bumpout bays totaling 600 sq. ft. of new space. No one room became huge, but the whole house seemed to expand at its core.

At the front of the house, the old one-story addition was torn off and a new two-story addition built 2½ ft. closer to the street, enlarging the living room and making space for an entry, powder room, and gallery hall downstairs. Upstairs, this addition created a bumpout in the boy's room, the roof over the entry, a laundry closet and bathroom, and a new room—the library—with its meditation loft and crow's nest–balcony under the eaves, overlooking the nearby salt marsh.

The two-story rear addition, though simpler, took more time to design. Not only did the architect want to preserve as much of the

A window-filled bay (part of a two-story addition) expands the son's bedroom on the front of the house.

A high ceiling gives the modest-sized library a soaring quality. The meditation loft is the highest livable spot in the house, nestling under the roofline, with its crow's-nest balcony offering a view of the salt marsh. On the other side of the room, a lowered ceiling over the couch gives that corner a cozy feeling.

Great Moves

Not only did rooms gain square footage, but they also became more open, especially in the downstairs where removing walls opened up the kitchen, dining room, and living room into one great room. Functional areas are defined with subtle clues, giving them identity and establishing boundaries. A one-step level change, for example, separates the dining room from the kitchen, straddled by an island. Living and dining rooms are separated by two simple wood posts where a wall used to be.

Along with open space comes shared noise, which makes it essential also to provide a quiet place. That's what the family room is for. It's one of the few downstairs rooms with a door, so kids can crank up the TV in there, or someone can escape inside for a little peace and quiet.

■ before and after ■

first floor

before

after

second floor

before

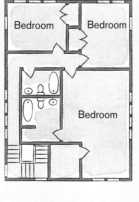

after

The open kitchen has a serene, natural color palette that contrasts nicely with the rich cabinetry of anigre wood and Brazilian cherry wood floors. A backsplash of hand-made 3-in.-square ceramic tile fits the scale of the space. Countertops are seaweed granite.

small backyard as possible, but zoning restrictions also limited the size of the footprint, leaving not much space to play with. Here, another two-story addition soars skyward, encompassing a mud-room off the kitchen, a deck adjoining the dining and family rooms downstairs, and a 3½-ft. by 9-ft. bumpout that expands the girl's bedroom on the second floor. A walk-in closet and sundeck are cantilevered off the master bedroom upstairs.

Relocating the Entry

A big flaw in the original layout was that there wasn't a separate entry. As in many post-World War II houses, the front door opened directly onto the living room, making it both a foyer and a circula-tion route to the heart of the home. Clearly, the house needed a transitional place for taking off boots, hanging up coats, and greet-ing guests with quiet welcome.

as it was ...

Know Your Passions

A S AN AVANT-GARDE artist with little interest in a traditional approach, Mindy Green knew from the onset she wanted a different, edgy house. She never wavered in that desire and was smart enough to hire an architect who understood what she wanted and didn't mind working collaboratively—for this transformation is truly a collaborative effort.

Whether you love it or you hate it (neighbors take both sides), the house doesn't fail to inspire. "Dare to be different," it shouts. The lesson: Sometimes it's okay not to marry new with existing in a perfect match. Go against the grain, if that's what you want to do.

The fireplace surround of African slate contains the entire earth-colored palette of the great room interior, helping to bring out the richness of the materials.

The new plan solves the problem in an interesting way, creating an entry vestibule of generous proportion for a small house. Located on the opposite side of the living room, the 140-sq.-ft. space (formed in part by a 6-ft. by 10-ft. two-story addition) contains an unusual architectural feature—a sinuous wall bordering a short hallway that serves as an art gallery as well as a path guiding visitors to the large main floor public area. By closing off the old entrance, the living room becomes whole; it doesn't have to behave like an entry or a hallway anymore. Windows replace the doorway, creating a good connection with the street.

A wavy wall leading from the entry hall to the living room creates a sense of anticipation—visitors wonder what they'll find around the corner.

as it was ...

A Radically Different Exterior

Mindy wanted a dramatically modern exterior, something abstract, like her paintings. Given the multiple additions in various parts of the house, she and Stein decided not to avoid the reality that the existing house would poke out here and there. They settled on a color and collage approach that gives a fractured, cubist quality to the exterior, with each piece expressing itself in subtle variations of material and color.

Borrowed Light

Rooms buried deep within a house tend to be dark, especially in old houses. When you take down walls to open up a plan, light from the sunny side penetrates deeper into the house, brightening once-dark spaces. Architects call this illuminating bonus "borrowed light."

The Greens' house has a relatively small footprint, so it wasn't difficult to borrow light. Every face of the house has good exposure. A good example occurs in the upstairs bathroom, where a partial wall is finished in glass block, permitting privacy while still ushering in diffuse light from the window-filled library across the hall. The library (with its aluminum ship's ladder leading to a meditation loft) is fitted with a ribbed glass door, so even when the door is closed the adjacent bathroom benefits from borrowed light.

Three parts of the house come together at this corner, giving the house an interesting outside-reflects-inside dimension. The wide clapboard section expands the living room and an upstairs bedroom; the narrow clapboard low piece is part of the original house; and the wood shingle tower expands the second-floor library with a galvanized-steel balcony cantilevered off the loft.

as it was ...

The long, narrow family room (decorated in a playful palette of black, white, and red) is designed for dual function—a TV viewing space at one end and a quieter game table space at the other end.

Using a palette familiar to the area (shingle and clapboard siding), the fractured composition creates an exciting, jazzy rhythm announcing, "Here's the old house! Here's the new!" A weathered shingle porch and entry tuck into the corner at the front of the house in thoughtful contrast to adjacent painted clapboard. An addition of the same scale and weathered shingle siding climbs the rear façade. Simple shed roofs with extending overhangs leap skyward to create an exciting level of detail where detail is often overlooked.

When doing something so radically different, it's important to remember context. This house relates to its neighborhood in the choice of shingle siding, the most prevalent siding used along the Connecticut coast. Given the curious juxtaposition of forms, it's the shingles that place the house firmly in its New England seashore setting.

A Craftsman Garage and Office

The 1940s single story ranch Robert Mahrer and Diana Vaniotis purchased in Santa Cruz, Calif., was a far cry from their dream house, but it had potential. A general building contractor by trade, Robert is often called upon to make a silk purse out of a sow's ear, and now he had the chance to do the same for his own home.

The long, narrow 1,100-sq.-ft. stucco structure sits 50 ft. back from the street on its 75-ft. by 100-ft. lot. Over the years, the couple had made cosmetic changes to the two-bedroom/one-bath house, always keeping in mind a major transformation down the road, when they had the time and the money. When Robert decided to move his office back home, the time arrived to make a definite plan.

WISH LIST

Build in the Craftsman style with handmade detailing

Build a new garage

Accommodate a separate office adjacent to the house

Add a large workshop

as it is today

French doors under the 9-ft.-tall office ceiling provide an indoor/outdoor connection to the balcony. The floor is vertical-grain Douglas fir.

Where New Meets Old

Before building the new addition, Mahrer upgraded the existing house, replacing aluminum windows with wood ones, upgrading interior doors with solid four-panel fir doors, adding custom moldings (including baseboards and a six-piece crown molding of his own design), and replacing exterior window and door surrounds with trim he designed and made in his shop. He carried these details through in the new addition, using a light plaster on the walls to match the texture found in the walls of the existing house. A breezeway (containing laundry and utility rooms, as well as access to the courtyard) connects the house with the garage/office.

From the street, the remodeled property is replete with interesting details. The fanciful garage/office introduces a Craftsman theme, while the detailing in the open, Japanese-inspired fence is repeated in the arbor, providing continuity.

Robert wanted a separate building for his office to keep work from interfering with daily life. The natural place to put it was in a garage addition close to the street where it would shield the house from passersby. That seed of an idea germinated into a whole-house transformation that would be accomplished in phases. Phase one, building the garage/workshop/office, set the tone for what would follow—saving the existing garage for a kitchen expansion in phase two.

Squeezing In under the Eaves

Phase one involved design and construction of an L-shaped story-and-a-half addition—a three-car garage with an office in the attic, attached to the house by a breezeway. Designed for two, the office is tucked into the roof in order to get two stories of living space without having the look of a tall building that would appear out of proportion with the single-story house. Whereas the roof of a typical two-story structure starts about 17 ft. above the concrete slab, the roof on this garage begins 11 ft. above the slab. The steep 10-in-12

To keep the roofline as low as possible, interior attic walls are only 4 ft. high. Headroom carved out for a gable dormer creates a sheltered space for a desk flanked by cabinets.

pitch of the gable roof allows more interior living space than a shallower pitched roof would. When combined with the two dormers (a gable dormer with the same 10-in-12 pitch on the front and a shed dormer with a shallower 4-in-12, pitched roof on the rear), the attic contains 490 sq. ft. of usable floor space.

Inside, 4-ft.-high walls create space for built-in desks and cabinetry, which wrap around the room and give plenty of headroom under the cathedral ceiling in the center. Sloping ceilings flatten off

Drywall follows the differing angles of the roof pitch, lending subtle sculptural form to the interior. Wrapping cabinets and desks around the perimeter of the room, where walls are the shortest, makes the most of the sloping ceilings.

Great Moves

Because the house sits back 50 ft. from the street, the logical place to put the new garage/office was in between the house and the street, providing privacy for the house and a public face for the business. The new 795-sq.-ft. three-car garage has a load-bearing wall dividing the single-car side from the double-car space, which is used as a workshop. Two doors open to the office stairs—one from the porch and walkway off the sidewalk and one from the workshop, so clients and employees can come and go without invading the family's privacy.

■ before and after ■

first floor

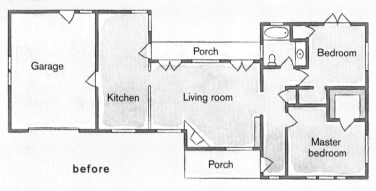

Garage

Kitchen

Porch

Living room

Bedroom

Porch

Master bedroom

before

Future family room

Kitchen and dining

Laundry

Covered patio

Bedroom

Living room

Master bedroom

Courtyard with pond

Front porch

Office porch with stream

Two-car garage/shop

Single-car garage

after

second floor

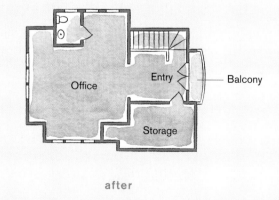

Office

Entry

Balcony

Storage

after

Flat-panel stairway balusters in the office (made out of black walnut and recycled vertical-grain Douglas fir) incorporate a traditional Craftsman dragonfly motif, which Mahrer uses as a business logo.

at the 9-ft. level, allowing heating and electrical runs to be hidden out of sight above the ceiling.

Finishing with Craftsman Details

Although he builds all styles of houses, Mahrer has always been partial to the Craftsman cottage style. He likes the handcrafted details, woodwork only a skilled craftsperson can do. Like Greene and Greene and other early 20th-century Arts and Crafts pioneers, Mahrer designs and manages construction of his projects, handling every detail from framing to built-ins to lighting and furnishings. He fashions much of the woodwork himself, making templates, cutting out shapes, fitting pieces together. When it came time to build and furnish his own workshop/office, he chose to do it in the spirit of the Arts and Crafts movement, combining natural local materials with his own ideas and skills.

Detailing began with the rafter tails, a curved cutout in the shape of a breaking wave, a nod to his passion for surfing. That led to other features—handcut dovetail joints on the corners where beams meet; corbels supporting the roof overhang, mimicking those on the back of the house; and lots of elliptical curves—in the gable ends, in

Instead of nails, porch beams are joined with hand-made dovetail joints. Simple corbels mimic those found elsewhere on the house. Rafter tails are designed to look like a breaking wave.

Handcrafted Garage Doors

Designed to look like traditional carriage doors that slide or swing open, the doors to the street-facing garage actually roll up and are operated by an electronic opener. They're fashioned from hollow plywood sections insulated with rigid foam and overlaid with 1x3 tongue-and-groove fir flooring with a V-groove routed between each board. A hand-rubbed oil finish gives the wood doors depth. Windows are seedy glass, typically used in stained-glass work, distorted with small bubbles for an old-time look.

Like a bridge, a window-filled breezeway connects the garage/office to the house and is directly accessible to the courtyard.

the fence, on the balcony. In places, the shape becomes a compound elliptical curve in an S-shape, adding movement and visual interest.

Creating an Outdoor Courtyard

As the design progressed, a courtyard evolved in the space between the addition and the house. Robert and Diana didn't want to look out on a blank wall, so they explored various options to add interest to this 11-ft.-wide by 20-ft.-long outdoor space. Some type of water

An 8-ft.-tall natural stone waterfall cascades into a 400-gal. concrete pond in the courtyard, which is visible from the living room, kitchen, and breezeway. The waterfall is a calming influence in both sight and sound.

A serendipitous element that evolved from a mistake, a little stream filled with stepping stones meanders directly in front of the office entrance, one of the most delightful features of the new addition.

feature seemed to be the best solution. As time went by, the plan grew, eventually taking form as an 8-ft.-high stone waterfall cascading into a 400-gal. pond made with 1-ft.-thick concrete walls veneered with small pebbles and capped with a stone rim.

Originally, all the water pumped through the filter went to the waterfall. To pump enough flow to keep the pond clear, the volume was too high for the waterfall and water splashed everywhere, including all over the French doors in the breezeway. At first, Mahrer thought he'd have to add another outlet pipe from the pump and filter (located underneath the office stairs) to the pond. Then he hit upon a better solution: simply running excess water into a small stream that trickles by the office door. This "mistake" has become his favorite feature of the pond.

A Vermont
Classic for Today

Open up the floor plan

Create a generous kitchen
and dining room

Provide good flow for
entertaining

Improve the indoor/
outdoor connection

Accommodate a family bath
and two bedrooms on the
second floor

From the outside, this simple farmhouse looks like a typical 19th-century structure in rural Vermont—staid, straitlaced, and spare. But inside a different story unfolds. Small surprises, eye-catching architectural details, and glorious colors give the interior a warm domesticity and sense of playfulness well suited to 21st-century family living.

The house sits on 55 acres purchased in 1940 as a summer retreat by Pi Smith's grandparents. Located in the Connecticut River Valley overlooking the mountains of New Hampshire, the property is classic rural New England with a big barn, sloping meadow, and gnarly old apple trees—a world away from the frenetic pace of urban Boston a two-hour drive away.

as it is today

New triple windows and a glazed door bring much-needed light into the living room. The sliding barn door, painted a deep cobalt blue, helps point the way to the entry.

The front façade facing the road was left as it has been for the last century and a half—with no new windows, the same roofline with matching parallel gables, and a simple white exterior.

as it was ...

Exterior changes were restricted to the rear of the house where several new windows and skylights were added. The sliding barn door was painted blue in a bold, playful stroke.

Built out of recycled posts and beams around 1840, the house is a typical regional style known as kneewall Cape, essentially one story with short 3-ft. 8 in. sidewalls on the second floor, allowing limited headroom and no light upstairs. A simple pitched roof is the style's most distinguishing characteristic, long and low without dormers or other roof features.

Like other historic houses in northern New England, the original portion was a rectangular timber-frame block, 22 ft. by 30 ft., consisting of four rooms with a center stair. A few years after it was built, a long, narrow ell with a parallel ridge was added to the west gable end. Originally, the ell contained the farm kitchen and a long woodshed with sliding barn doors on both sides—an unheated, windowless space for farmers to split wood and do other chores. In 1980, Pi's father converted the ell into a living room and opened it up to the kitchen.

Revamping the Old Structure

When Pi (an architect) inherited the property, the first-floor structure of the original rectangle was completely rotten and wildly out of level, sloping 6 in. from one corner of the kitchen to the other. Poor heat, no insulation, and leaky windows made the entire house uncomfortably chilly in winter. The awkward layout of rooms and the small, inefficient kitchen were sources of constant frustration for Pi and her partner, Ann Bumpus, who enjoy entertaining. Dropped ceilings hid picturesque post-and-beam framing, making the ceilings undesirably low. The stair and second-floor bedrooms were dark. A total renovation was in order to open up the floor plan, bring in more light, and create a stronger connection to the beautiful landscape.

For Pi, the design challenge became a matter of reconciling opposites: balancing Vermont vernacular architecture with her modernist upbringing and training, and keeping the spirit of the 19th-century farmhouse of her childhood alive while creating a

A change in ceiling height signals the transition from the oldest portion of the house to the ell. An interior window at the roof's peak opens onto a child's playroom, providing a glimpse of the second story while sharing light.

Interior walls were knocked down to open up the entire first floor, creating long views through the house to give a feeling of spaciousness. Here, a 4-ft. wall segment framed by a rough post visually separates the kitchen/dining area from the living room without blocking the view.

Exterior changes were restricted to the rear of the house, where several new windows and skylights were added. The sliding barn door was painted blue in a bold, playful stroke.

colorful, cheerful environment inside. With the owner's limited budget and 2,200 sq. ft. to work with, the house didn't need any more space, it just needed to make better use of the space it had. Pi wanted to keep the historic simple gable form, so she decided to work within the existing footprint.

Opening Up the Interior

Opening up the plan was priority number one. Interior walls were knocked down, creating long views so that wherever you stand you catch a glimpse of other rooms. From the front door, you can see all the way though the house. To keep the front façade exactly as it has been for more than a century, all window changes were relegated to the back of the house, away from the road, where two banks of three divided-light windows flood the interior with natural light. Old windows and flat-panel doors were retained to offer contrast between the old house and the clean lines of new detailing.

Subtle room separations help define living areas, allowing spaces to flow and overlap with each other. For example, the dining room is effectively defined by a 4-ft. wall with a post, which gives it a corner without closing it off. The kitchen overlaps both living and dining spaces, allowing for easy communication with family members and guests and visual supervision of a busy toddler.

The farmhouse and rustic barn (left) sit on 55 rural acres overlooking a sloping meadow with a view toward the mountains of New Hampshire.

Because the kitchen lacks overhead cabinets, finding space for storage was a trick. Deep floor-to-ceiling storage was accomplished with an extra-thick wall shared with the stairway, permitting the refrigerator to be set flush with the countertops and providing space for an extra-deep pantry closet and cabinet.

The kitchen island (left) is designed in a graceful arc to eliminate the sharp points of 90-degree angles. A single bracket, long and simple, supports the overhanging cherry top at its broadest point.

In this corner next to the refrigerator, a deep cabinet is set back under the stair and brought down within 8 in. of the kitchen counter to maximize storage. Instead of a typical 25-in.-deep counter, this is a 9-in.-deep ledge, creating a pleasant workstation that visually ties the cabinetry together.

THE SEVEN

Know Your Palette

ON THE EXTERIOR, the old farmhouse remains a simple, neutral white, as it has for more than a century, fitting in with other houses along the road. A sliding barn door, painted blue for a bold, playful touch, is the only exception.

Inside, a mixture of old-house funkiness and modern sophistication prevails. A rich palette of interwoven color and texture allows notched posts and beams to stand out, becoming a sculptural element. Each of the principal spaces on the first floor is a different color, helping reinforce their separateness, but the palette as a whole (ochre, terra-cotta, muted greens with black accents) is richly harmonious, so colors layer beautifully as you look through the length of the house. Contrasting with these earth tones, second-floor colors are airy and springlike—cobalt blues and greens with bright white trim.

Because the kitchen is central and highly visible from the living and dining rooms, Pi wanted to use as few wall cabinets as possible and to have the casework either be tailored, "tucked in," or sculptural. Minimizing cabinets allowed the outside wall to be almost entirely windows, opening up the kitchen to outside views.

Two additional design strategies—variation of ceiling heights and color treatments—define each space within the open plan. A cathedral ceiling soars 15 ft. to the ridgeline in the ell, creating a lofty living room with its hearth, woodstove, and large wall of floor-to-ceiling bookcases. Original rough-hewn beams (once covered by lath and plaster) are exposed with rough tinted plaster infill—higher (8½ ft.) over the hearth and kitchen; lower (7½ ft.) over the dining room. Upstairs, Pi took advantage of unused attic space to lift ceilings to the ridgeline, exposing collar ties and adding skylights, thus transforming two stuffy, under-lit bedrooms into small but airy, expansive spaces.

Rerouting the Stair

Other than taking down most of the first-floor walls, the single most transformative architectural move was to relocate the stair. Before, a dark-walled tunnel divided the house in two, making it impossible to create a generous dining room on the first floor and forcing circulation patterns to the outside edges of the house (a problem especially on the second floor with its limited headroom under the roof).

On the first floor, a wall of books goes up to an old beam and stops, separating the living room from the office. A triangular loft atop the office (created by the cathedral ceiling and reached by a ladder) slips in under the eaves and is open to the living room below.

Great Moves

Before renovation, the old layout of small rooms with many doorways and lots of wasted circulation space cried out to be opened up and modernized. The agenda called for removing and changing walls, adding windows, and rerouting the staircase.

All changes occurred within the existing footprint of the house. The house didn't grow at all, though it now feels spacious and efficient. Relocating the stair solved a myriad of problems, creating space for an open kitchen/dining area downstairs; permitting traffic to arrive in the center of the second floor, and making it possible to access two bedrooms and a bath off a small upstairs hall. Part of the area formerly occupied by the stair was reclaimed for a shower and bath linen storage under the eaves. Downstairs, spaces flow and overlap with one another. The guest room (originally larger) became a guest suite with the addition of a bath and laundry room.

■ before and after ■

first floor

second floor

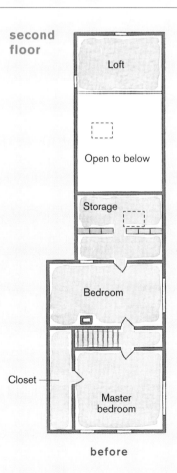

A new switchback stair, pushed to the north side of the house, allowed the first floor to be opened up and permitted traffic to arrive in the center of the second floor, making it possible to create a center hall with doors to two bedrooms and a bathroom. The configuration of the stair, with the upper run ascending with the roofline, takes advantage of the Cape form.

Aesthetically, the stair has two important features. It angles, broadening as you enter the dining room, to create an embracing opening. This angled wall is extra thick, allowing modulation of space on either side. On the kitchen side, the thick wall creates space deep enough to bury the refrigerator so it sits flush with the kitchen cabinets. On the stair side, the thick wall allows placement of an internal window so upstairs light now spills into the kitchen. The stair landing—with its rough-hewn beams and little niche—becomes a calm space between floors.

To make the most of available space under the roof, built-in cabinets and a long shelf are tucked under the angled ceiling in the family bath, reserving the tallest portion of the room for the vanity and a wall of mirrors.

Small Moves

Create Kneewall Storage

To make the second-floor rooms under the sloping roof feel more comfortable and raise the perceived headroom, internal kneewalls were built a couple of feet in from the exterior wall in both the bathroom and the master bedroom headboard wall.

This accomplishes two things: Ceilings don't get so low that you're in danger of bumping your head, and welcome storage space is created at the edges. Behind the bed, otherwise low, useless space was turned into a cascading bookshelf headboard. In the bathroom, cabinets hug the kneewall, leaving higher ceiling areas for standing at the sinks and accessing the tub and shower.

The hearth is made of the same materials as the kitchen backsplash, only here tiles are broken and placed in a mosaic incorporating tiny square glazed tiles. Everything else is multicolored slate containing the entire color palette of the first floor.

Where New Meets Old

Modern meets rustic in the kitchen where shiny stainless-steel appliances, clean lines, and simple detail add a contemporary touch against the notched and gouged timber framework. The ceiling is higher over the kitchen than in the dining room, marking the transition between the oldest section of the house and the ell. Strong horizontal lines—such as the countertops and the backsplash tile capped with cherry—help tie the room together.

Delightful Details

Unconventional architectural details create a wealth of delight inside—the angled stair, a gently curving kitchen island with an elongated bracket, a tiered and angled spice rack built between ancient notched posts. An artful mosaic of multicolored slate and tiny glazed tile decorates the kitchen backsplash, repeated in another pattern at the living room hearth. Repetition of these small but key design elements lends a thread of continuity between the rooms, tying them together in a cohesive design, a necessity in an open plan where each room flows into the next.

Upstairs, whimsical details appear in the baby's bedroom and playroom. What was once a low, dreary attic is now a delightful, brightly colored extension of the baby's bedroom—complete with swirling hanging rod brackets and decorative paintings. The slanted roofline offers adults a mere 4-ft. width of standing space, whereas a toddler can easily poke around in 15 ft. side to side. Triangular bookcases divide the bedroom from the playroom, making the most of low space at the eaves. A new skylight brings in light and air, and a small pair of shuttered windows open onto the living room below, creating rich possibilities for play and a visual connection to the rest of the house.

A child's playroom upstairs is painted a happy mix of earth and sky colors, providing excellent contrast for the primary colors of a toddler's toys. The shuttered interior window overlooks the living room and gives a straight-ahead view to the loft at the end of the ell.

Small details in the child's bedroom and play area set a whimsical mood. Here, a swirling rosette is used in a decorative way to hold a closet rod.

From the beginning, the renovation was planned for economy. Important expensive-to-relocate features were kept in their original locations (woodstove, kitchen, washer/dryer). Wherever possible, items were rescued and reused: windows, an old claw-foot tub, hemlock and pine flooring. To stay within budget, compromises were made: The bathroom counter is maple instead of stone, and kitchen countertops are Fireslate®, an industrial material available at a fraction of the cost of real stone.

A Small, Multifunctional Add-On

- Create a comfortable gathering spot
- Include bookshelves and "away space" for reading
- Add a mudroom
- Make sure the design fits the character of the house
- Provide a connection to the outdoors

JoAnne and David Alkire had big ambitions for a not-so-big addition. With two small children and a third on the way, they were outgrowing their small house in Minneapolis. The first floor of the boxy 1949 Colonial Revival structure consisted of a small kitchen and an open living room-dining room area. Upstairs, a bath and three bedrooms squeezed into a 24-ft. by 28-ft. space. There was nowhere in the 1,350-sq.-ft. house to spread out, nowhere to stake out a bit of personal "space," no gathering place for the family, no casual place to entertain friends. There was just a postage stamp-size entryway to take off outdoor gear and no place to put it all.

The Alkires wanted an affordable rear addition that would fix all those problems. They asked architect Robert Gerloff for a master bedroom and bath upstairs and a new first-floor space encompassing a reading nook, shelves for JoAnne's book collection, a place for David to sit with friends

as it is today

Designed for versatility and space efficiency, these built-ins combine a full-depth desk with standard 12-in.-deep cabinets, drawers, and shelves. Gerloff reserved room for windows above the display ledge. The shelves continue the pattern of horizontal bands in the doors and sidelights.

Horizontal lines visually widen the addition. The upper siding, white trim, large bay, and gentle roof pitch echo the look of the house, while the bay's flat roof and off-center window divider make a new statement.

and watch sports on television, a family computer center, a mudroom, a pantry, pleasing views, lots of sunlight, and much better access to the outdoors.

Gerloff designed a 16-ft. by 24-ft., two-story add-on with bedroom and bath above. The eye-opener is the first floor, which contains a multipurpose "cozy room" and a mudroom.

One Room, Many Uses

Gerloff dubbed the new room a "cozy room" for good reason. The 275-sq.-ft. living space is a bright yet intimate room enveloped by windows, built-ins, and warm red walls. Several activity areas share the sun and views, but they occupy separate quadrants of the room.

The computer area, with painted wood desk and cabinets recalling Colonial features, lines one wall. Coordinating bookcases on the opposite wall frame an opening for the television. A sofa and soft

Although centered off the back of the house, the bay is closer to the bookshelves inside the "cozy room," where it works as a reading nook or seating space around the television. Squaring off the bay yields maximum window exposure and floor area.

The sunny mudroom piggybacks onto the side of the cozy room, offering generous space for built-in lockers and a pantry. The linoleum floor, which continues into the kitchen, recalls the rectangular shapes of the traditional house but adds an exciting twist. The glass door and sidelights duplicate those on the cozy room.

chairs circle around this wall, forming a comfy place for the family to watch a movie, or for David and friends to take in the Final Four. Although the soft chairs face into the room, they nestle inside a glass-wrapped box bay where JoAnne can slip away to read or drink in the garden view.

A mudroom runs the full depth of the addition from the back door to the kitchen. Just inside the door, locker-style cabinets with hooks and adjustable shelves help keep everybody's gear handy and organized. A sleek, plank shelf doubles as a bench and a table for bags and briefcases. Wide, closed cabinets are an extension of the adjacent kitchen; JoAnne uses them as a pantry to store small appliances, canned goods, and other things that were bulging out of the kitchen before.

Small Space That Looks and Feels Bigger

Gerloff carefully observed the house's stylistic traditions of symmetry and restraint, but he tossed in a few carefree surprises. One is a fun, quirky, off-center window divider in the bay. Another is the linoleum floor that streams through the mudroom and kitchen, displaying a vibrant pattern of giant parallelograms that visually expands the space.

A deep overhang shields the mudroom stoop so the owners can get out of the weather, while the sidelight makes the entry feel wide and welcoming.

Great Moves

Gerloff used a deep roof overhang to shade the west-facing bay and even deeper overhangs to shelter the doorways flanking it. In fact, the doorway overhangs are as deep as the bay and stretch to the corners of the addition, covering 4-ft. by 7-ft. entry stoops that are big enough for the whole family to huddle out of the rain or snow as they unlock the door. The Alkires love this luxury.

■ before and after ■

first floor

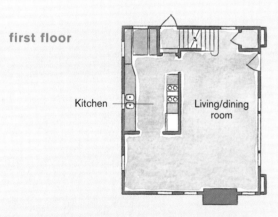

Kitchen — Living/dining room

before

Kitchen
Mudroom — Entry
"Cozy room" — Living room
Dining room

after

second floor

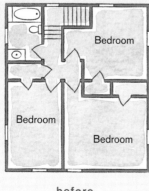

Bedroom
Bedroom
Bedroom

before

Bedroom
Master bedroom
Guest bedroom
Bedroom

after

To make the cozy room feel bigger, Gerloff emphasized light and circulation. The more sources of natural light a room has, the bigger it feels, and the cozy room draws sunlight from all around. Light comes from large windows on the back wall and around the bay; from high windows over the computer center; from the frosted-glass pocket door to the mudroom; and from French doors to the window-rich dining room. Circulation options also expand space, and the cozy room has lots of those, with access to the dining room, mudroom, and backyard.

Gerloff maximized floor area both by popping out the bay and by incorporating the desk and television shelf into the cabinetry. Horizontal bands of shelving, window, and door trim visually elongate the walls of the cozy room. Outside, Gerloff balanced the vertical thrust of columns and trim with strong horizontal lines. A flat roof, uncharacteristic of a Colonial house, bisects the addition and suggests that something new and different has been added. Above it are wide-board siding and double-hung windows that match the existing house. Below are narrower lap siding, the horizontally banded sidelights and doors, and that bay window that calls out to be noticed and enjoyed.

Building a television cabinet into the bookshelf keeps the TV from dominating the room. Since the garage is in prominent view from the cozy room, Gerloff dressed it up with trelliswork. The garage door looks just like the mudroom door across the yard.

Contemporary behind a Formal Façade

WISH LIST

Create a smooth link between old and new

Open up sight lines through the house

Add a master bedroom suite with quiet, getaway space

Provide a feeling of connection to the outside

As a remodeling contractor, Scott Henningsen may have had a sixth sense about the 1922 foursquare he and his wife, Kelly Mooney, spotted in their search for a suburban house. This one had a certain old-fashioned charm and was located in a neighborhood outside Columbus, Ohio, that was an ideal place to raise kids. But the house was run-down, dark, and, at 1,400 sq. ft., way too small for their family of four.

At first Kelly thought Scott was kidding when he wanted to buy the property. But after they brainstormed about revamping the interior and building a rear addition, she was as enthusiastic as Scott. They bought the house, brought it up to current code standards, and infused it with light and life.

The original house was a basic box with walled-off rooms. The first floor contained a parlor, dining room, entry

Gray siding, white trim, and harmonious rooflines blend new with old without mimicry. But narrow siding and horizontal windows distinguish the main addition; the tree room stands out even more, with vertical board and batten siding, trapezoidal windows, and a different shade of gray.

Well equipped for the family's comings and goings, the mudroom bumpout includes slide-out baskets that stow hats and gloves and a drop-off counter for backpacks and purses. A partial wall helps hide the clutter.

hall, and modest kitchen. There was no first-floor bathroom. On the second floor, a narrow, meandering hallway threaded past three small bedrooms and a bathroom. The attic offered a patch of usable space under the eaves.

Scott and Kelly wanted to break out of that box, enlarging the house substantially with a two-story addition and opening up the existing rooms with a more free-flowing design. The idea was to create an imaginative, light-filled space that, while contemporary, still respected the character of the old house. They wanted the first floor to be a comfortable, friendly place for the family as well as a handsome setting for entertaining. The second floor needed elbow room for both kids plus a master bedroom sanctuary. Architect Jonathan Barnes came up with a design that does it all, with a nod to the existing house and a wink to the many playful new features.

The construction was done by Scott's company, H Construction, Ltd. The first step was to cut off the back wall and attach a 1,100-sq.-ft.

Know Your Place

SCOTT AND KELLY wanted to add excitement to their house without jarring the rhythm of the traditional old neighborhood. That's why, from the front, the remodeled house still looks much like the other foursquares on the street. Subtle changes along the sides of the house suggest a transition to something new, but the addition lets loose with wild creativity only in back and out of general view.

The roof of the main addition is flush with the existing roof, and the quirky tree room roof is hidden from the street. Siding and trim in similar patterns and colors smoothly blend new with old, while a darker gray wall pocket (which houses a downspout) marks the start of the addition. It's the addition's innovative side windows, arranged in horizontal bands placed high in the wall, that hint of surprises in store.

Great Moves

Less is definitely more where ceilings are removed to open up the house with airy spaces and sunny shafts. In the remodeled entryway, the ceiling has been removed to create a bright, bold space that soars two stories. Little was lost upstairs—just a section of stair landing—and an existing second-floor window becomes a dramatic sun catcher for the space below. A cross-beam remains, lending both structural support and design vitality.

■ before and after ■

first floor

Mudroom

Deck

Kitchen

Dining room

Kitchen

Dining room

Living room

Parlor

Den

Entry

Entry

Porch

Porch

before

after

second floor

Tree room

Master bedroom

Bedroom

Closet

Laundry

Bedroom

Bedroom

Bedroom

Hall

Hall

Bedroom

Bedroom

Open to below

before

after

A view through the house from the front door adds drama and makes the house feel larger. The two-story-high entry is flooded with light from first- and second-story windows and the landing window; cherry flooring warms the space.

Removing a ceiling section opened the entry and made a more airy, spacious stairway. It also revealed a structural beam, which has been detailed to match other trim and is an interesting architectural feature in its own right.

addition. The main floor of the new space includes a living room, kitchen, mudroom, and deck. Overhead are a master bedroom and bathroom, and a quirky, inventive getaway that Scott and Kelly call their "tree room." Most of the original kitchen area was used for a half bath, closet, and basement stairway. Reconfiguring the existing second floor made room for a laundry room, attic staircase, kids' bathroom, and the master bedroom walk-in closet.

Opening Up the First Floor

The addition energizes the first floor of the house with an infusion of daylight, open spaces, and expansive views. The dramatic transformation is announced at the front entry, where the foyer ceiling has been removed to create a tower of sunlight overhead, and views extend all the way through the house to the backyard. A freestanding fireplace box topped by a chic, concrete countertop marks the border between the existing dining room and the addition. With no confining walls, movement and space-expanding views flow freely from the front door all the way through the house to the trees beyond.

Next to the fireplace, four steps lead down to the addition. Placing the addition's floor lower than the existing main floor not only created a sense of arrival where new meets old. It also gave the new space a lofty, 11-ft. ceiling without affecting the floors on the second floor. Sets of extra-wide French doors open to the patio, which is level with the living room. All the doors can be opened when company comes, smoothly extending the entertainment space to the outdoors. A few steps down from the patio is a lower section of patio that penetrates farther into the landscaped yard.

Within the addition, a large peninsula counter marks the border—and link—between the living room and kitchen. When company comes, the peninsula becomes a bridge to the living

The fireplace box with painted stovepipe and concrete countertop forms a half-wall that gracefully resolves the difference between the floor heights of the dining room and the new, lower living room.

Two sets of French doors lead from the living room to the patio with no change in floor level, easing the connection to the outdoors. A high band of side windows yields wall space for furniture and maintains privacy.

To create a rimless sink that is easy to clean and looks pretty, Scott had the ready-made stainless-steel sink welded into the steel peninsula counter. He made the concrete perimeter counters himself. Both counter-tops mix well with the contemporary, maple cabinetry.

The sculptural counter is the work center of the kitchen and a gathering place for family and friends. The fireplace seamlessly links the original dining room and the new, lower living room. Views between spaces enrich and visually enlarge the house.

Broad painted bands in the den create a smart-looking pattern that's subtler and easier to replace than wallpaper. Scott sandblasted the glass on the old cabinet doors to obscure from view what's stored on the shelves.

room. Guests can sit at the counter to chat while Scott and Kelly work in the kitchen. On most days, the counter functions as part of the kitchen, where the kids eat breakfast and meals are prepared.

Focus on Family Spaces

Scott and Kelly wanted the house to be pretty enough for company but practical enough for family living. They needed a way for the family to spread out yet feel connected. One answer was to turn the front parlor into a den that's nice enough for company but casual enough for the kids to hang out in. Double pocket doors can close the room for noise control. A new doorway, leading from the room to the service hallway, would have made the den too open, so Barnes yanked it from the plans. In its place is a 1-ft.-wide slot in the wall. Beginning 2 ft. above floor level, the slot gives parents and kids a visual connection between den and kitchen.

A 1-ft. by 4-ft. wall slot provides a visual connection between the den and the kitchen down the hall. The slot and the square cutout above it echo window shapes in the house.

Sleek Sliding Doors

Architect Jonathan Barnes used sliding doors to add aesthetic zest and save space otherwise hogged by swinging doors. In the master bedroom, handsome, maple veneer panels on simple industrial tracks form a wide bathroom entry and double doors to the walk-in closet. In the narrow downstairs hallway, three panels on two tracks conveniently glide over each other for access to the half bath, the adjacent pantry, and the basement entrance. Glazed pocket doors—cousins to sliders and original to the house—contain noise in the den without blocking sunlight and views.

Upstairs, the boy's bedroom at the front of the house seemed boxy and small. Since the attic space above it was unusable, Barnes uncapped the room and punched the ceiling up to the roof. Scott's third-floor office has an interior window overlooking his son's fun, tall room.

Because they added a master bedroom, Scott and Kelly could sacrifice one of the original bedrooms. They used part of the space for a second-floor laundry room, working on the theory that you might as well put the machines where most of the laundry is generated.

The dark upstairs hall was a narrow 28 in. wide. Scott and Kelly introduced a more gracious flow by widening the hall to 4 ft. Again, long views through to the tree room make the house feel larger. Sun filters through, lending light and cheer to the hall. And the intriguing tree room beckons.

Although small in area, the boy's bedroom is big in volume and pizzazz with a ceiling that rises to the roof peak. Painting the ceiling a light color adds brightness and lift to the room.

Close to Nature: The Tree Room

In the back of the house, out of general view, the house is playful and spirited. The master bedroom is light and lofty, with a cathedral ceiling, twin skylights, and big windows. The tree room takes the light and loftiness even further, wrapped in glass and jutting away from the house at a skewed angle to capture a 180-degree view. Walls tilt, the ceiling slopes, and trapezoidal windows rise toward an outer point. These features are gutsy, adventurous, and delightfully zany. Yet the natural wood finish, enriched by pine flooring salvaged from the attic floor, makes this cozy retreat as tranquil and alluring as an old-fashioned treehouse.

Bridging the boundary in space and style, a slim wall is trimmed to match the bedroom but playfully angled like the tree room.

as it was ...

Large windows and two skylights in the cathedral ceiling open the master bedroom to the outdoors. The tree room is even more outdoorsy; jutting away from the house, it feels as though it is in the trees.

Colonial
Transformation

Add a master bedroom suite with sitting room and bath

Freshen up the back porch

Give the exterior a facelift

This Connecticut Colonial started life as a rather plain 1970s builder's plan (the kind found in suburbs throughout the country), but you'd never know it today. An ambitious renovation, including a two-story addition and facelift with historic Colonial details, transformed this once boxy house into a grand homestead that looks as if it's been sitting on its site for more than 200 years.

When Jackie and Bill Bishop, the original owners, purchased the 3,000-sq.-ft. house, their children were small and the development the house was in was brand new. Over the years the house changed in minor ways to suit the needs of the growing family—the addition of a bumpout, a back porch, a kitchen remodeling. By the time the Bishops became empty nesters, the house was looking worn and drab and no longer suited the way they lived. But with lovingly maintained gardens, a secluded swimming pool, and 250 acres of

as it is today

A good way to make a small space look bigger is to use volume instead of square footage. Here, a cross gable allows a high-vaulted ceiling for spatial variety, providing a welcome break from 8-ft. ceilings in the rest of the house.

Where New Meets Old

Awide archway marks the spot where the addition meets the original building. The exterior wall was torn out in the bedroom and a 375-sq.-ft. addition built incorporating a sitting room and bath in two separate gables. The division of spaces transforms this relatively young house into a home with a period feel, maintaining a pattern of scale familiar to the owners and consistent with other rooms in the house.

After a facelift, the exact age of this Connecticut Colonial is hard to pin down. Is it an antique home or new? A proud main form and carefully selected window and column proportions provide historical reference. Narrow wood siding and a new hand-split shake roof make it look even more authentic.

natural woodland abutting their backyard, moving was out of the question. They'd rather renovate, bringing their family home up to the standards of the now-affluent neighborhood.

Looking at the finished house today, it's almost impossible to tell what is old and what is new. The exterior underwent a masterful transformation, making the house look more historic. Inside, cozy light-filled rooms nestle under a rustic sheltering roof.

Creating a Master Suite

The first item on the Bishops' wish list was a master suite. To accommodate the Bishops' request, architect Matthew Schoenherr devised an elegant solution—three modest rooms flowing one into the other, respecting the Colonial pattern of discrete rooms. An efficient 375-sq.-ft. addition to the second story links the sleeping chamber (the former bedroom) to a light-filled sitting room and master bath. Rather than add on in one big block, the new rooms each have their

A window next to the tub is a welcome feature where privacy is not an issue. This one is boxed out, allowing a 9-in.-deep windowsill to double as a tub-side shelf.

own gable—the sitting room in a cross gable overlooking the side yard, the bath off the main gable facing backyard gardens.

In the old bedroom, a 9-ft. bank of walk-in closets replaced the old master bath. The exterior wall was torn out and a wide archway built, opening the 13-ft. by 15-ft. space onto the first room of the addition—a similarly proportioned sitting room with traditional fireplace and French doors leading to a balcony. Off the sitting room, a 9-ft. by 13½-ft. bath contains all the elements of a full bath in a small space—shower, soaking tub, two sinks. A thick wall placed between the sitting room and bath creates the necessary depth to house the firebox and storage cabinets. Heating and air conditioning ducts fill leftover space.

The porch, designed for year-round use, contains an unexpected feature—a large centrally placed wood-burning fireplace fashioned out of rough local granite.

Converting a Porch into a Four-Season Room

With a new master bath upstairs, the porch below needed to be insulated to keep plumbing pipes from freezing. The old porch couldn't support a two-story addition anyway, so it was torn out and 42-in.-deep footings were dug for a new foundation, providing the perfect opportunity for a casual indoor/outdoor room.

The new four-season porch is L-shaped with a wide expanse of windows to bring in light and air. A massive central fireplace helps heat the space in winter, creating a cozy indoor porch with expansive views to the backyard and woodland. Large French doors open onto an adjoining terrace and path leading to the natural-stone pool.

Setting the addition back several feet from the existing house (standard practice in Colonial design) allowed two original windows to be retained and positioned the porch and terrace to access backyard gardens.

as it was ...

Small Moves

Custom-Made Windows and Screens

To keep the new indoor/outdoor porch open to summer breezes yet closed tight to retain heat during winter, windows have two sets of sashes. In winter, 20 fixed 5-ft.-tall glazed panels protect the room from freezing temperatures.

Screen panels replace them in summertime. Wood handles fastened to the sash make lifting the panels easy; they simply lift up and settle down into position. Glazed sash is a manufactured product whereas the jambs (frames) were custom-built on site.

Great Moves

A tall, narrow, two-story 800-sq.-ft. addition satisfies the Bishops' wish list. Upstairs, in the 375-sq.-ft. addition to the master bedroom, a sitting room and bath nestle under the gable roof. Downstairs, the old porch was replaced with a new L-shaped indoor/ outdoor room—425 sq. ft. of year-round living packed into a not-so-big space. Divided-light porch windows provide rhythm and scale consistent with older Colonial-style homes, while the flat roof of the porch serves as a balcony off the sitting room.

▪ before and after ▪

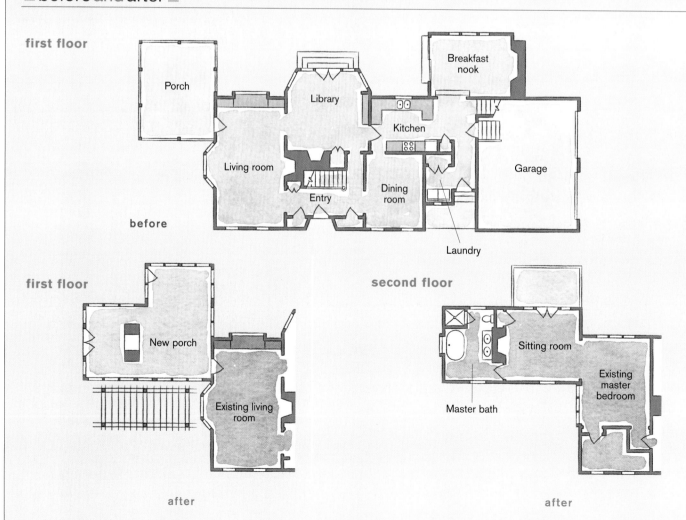

first floor

Porch

Library

Breakfast nook

Kitchen

Living room

Entry

Dining room

Garage

Laundry

before

first floor

New porch

Existing living room

after

second floor

Master bath

Sitting room

Existing master bedroom

after

Setting the addition several feet back from the main house is both a traditional feature and a practical one. The 14-ft. setback matches that of an earlier mudroom addition on the opposite side and allows two original windows on the first and second floors to be retained.

In keeping with the Colonial style, the two-story addition (four-season room below, master suite above) is modest in scale so it doesn't dwarf the main form. It's tall and narrow, presenting a proud appearance typical of New England architecture.

Upgrading the Exterior

Upgrading the home presented a good opportunity to tweak exterior details for a truer expression of early American heritage. At the same time, sturdy materials replaced weather-beaten ones. Energy-efficient windows (double-pane glazing in wood frames with wood muntin bars simulating authentic divided lights) were installed in place of drafty old windows. In some cases, windows were boxed out and capped with copper roofs to create deeper sills inside and break up the flat façade outside. The old asphalt roof was torn off and replaced with heavy, hand-split cedar shakes, the kind a historic Colonial would have.

New decorative details (reminiscent of Colonial Williamsburg) subtly dress up angled trim boards (known as rakes) beneath the roof shingles on gable ends around the house. Shutters screwed flat against the clapboards were replaced with working wood shutters hung on authentic operating hinges and held back with wrought-iron "shutter dogs" to give them a bold, three-dimensional appearance. Instead of a severe flat façade, a classically detailed portico now welcomes visitors, offering shelter from inclement weather. Attention to these types of details makes the house begin to look like an authentic historic Colonial home, one that's been sitting proudly on its Connecticut site for a few hundred years.

Classical details on the new portico (triple Tuscan columns, pilasters flanking the door, operable shutters with wrought-iron hardware, little gable decorated with crown molding) add a balanced formality to the symmetry of this home's Colonial design.

as it was …

Growing a Box
on a Budget

This whole-house transformation designed for an active family of seven was driven by the owners' desire to have five bedrooms and four baths. Originally a rundown 1,400-sq.-ft. single-story box built in 1952, the house is now an impressive 3,400-sq.-ft. two-story modern structure with a large great room and a professional office with private entrance. Half of the existing house was torn off and half remains, though it's almost impossible to tell where new meets old.

Architect Carol Cozen purchased the house for its location—a small beach community with clean air, excellent schools, and a family-oriented atmosphere. She was looking for a house that she and her husband, Matt Bernstein, could transform to fit their family of four children and live-in nanny. This house fit the bill—zoning permitted a full-time office, and the house was centrally located for Carol's southern California clientele.

The contemporary design is comprised of three distinct forms—a two-story wedge-shaped section with a sloping roof, a two-story rectangular block, and a connecting link housing the entry, stair, and library.

To make the small backyard look bigger, bamboo plants are pulled away from the fence to give an illusion of depth, creating a hidden walkway for the kids to play hide-and-go-seek. The office in the backyard setback has three exterior walls, making it feel like a separate wing.

Where New Meets Old

Half of the existing house was demolished and half incorporated into the new structure. Aside from the office (located in a former master suite), the only visible constant between new and old is the garage that stayed in its original position, taking up half of the front façade, a typical southern California gesture. To conform to earthquake code and support the second story, a 12-ft. by 18-ft. moment frame (two steel posts supporting a steel beam) surrounds the garage door.

A sheet of safety glass supported by two timber beams provides a minimalist awning above the front door. The glass in the door is sandblasted to allow privacy and diffuse light.

The deteriorating, nondescript structure left Carol free to design the home she wanted. Because the old house contained a nonconforming setback (a back room added before the passage of zoning laws), she gained a larger footprint than she would have if building new. Saving half of the tiny house cut foundation and lumber costs, too.

Fitting a Lot of Living on a Not-So-Big Lot

The big design challenge was how to fit a large home on a postage stamp-sized property—and do it on a tight budget. The 50-ft. by 90-ft. lot didn't leave much room to grow. A second story was definitely in order, but Carol didn't want it to shade the tiny backyard. Her solution was to design two distinct two-story forms with a connection in the middle, giving the whole structure a modern blocky appearance, then sloping the roofline of one section to permit a sunny backyard.

One architectural trick that makes this house live bigger is giving key rooms dual uses. For example, the upstairs hallway (the connecting link) is a library with floor-to-ceiling bookshelves. The front foyer doubles as a music room. The laundry/utility area is also a mail center and pet care station. Two daughters share a bedroom.

The 19-ft. by 25-ft. great room is the heart of the house—family room, living room, and playroom all in one, open to the kitchen and eating space so all public functions flow together into one unified

A mail-sorting center in the laundry room organizes mail for each member of the family. There are cubbies for each parent and the four children.

The open stair landing at the upper level connects the private wings and utilizes otherwise dead space as a library. A wall of maple bookshelves is punctuated with windows that allow daylight to shine through.

Exposed wood and metal trusses support the 1½-story roof over the great room. The fireplace is surrounded by concrete and topped by a stainless-steel angle bracket for a mantel. Flooring is sustainable bamboo with the texture of carpet.

Foundation, walls, and exposed ceiling joists in the studio are left over from a previous bedroom/bath, but the room received new windows, doors, and lighting. A floor of plywood sheeting kept finishing costs down.

To make the space as open as possible, a moment frame (two steel columns supporting a steel beam) spans the 9-ft. by 15-ft. opening between the dining room and kitchen.

A palette of white and light maple creates serene sleeping quarters in the master suite, enhanced by soft breezes blowing in from open sliding doors off the shallow balcony.

Clean towels stored in a door-less cubby help break up the mass of cabinetry in the master bath and are handy when needed.

whole. Varied ceiling heights keep the room from feeling cavernous, with a cathedral ceiling over an L-shaped section adjacent to the kitchen giving way to a lower ceiling over the more intimate fireplace sitting area. During the frequent dinner parties that the couple hosts (big events for 40 or more people), everyday furniture is moved to the garage and the room becomes a huge dining hall.

Carol's office (formerly a master suite) is located in a previous addition at the back of the house. Since three of the four walls are exterior walls, she had several options when placing the entrance. With an adjacent bath easily accessible, the 15-ft. by 17-ft. space doesn't feel like an integral part of the house, giving a professional appearance to both clients and employees.

Upstairs, bedrooms are zoned into wings—one for adults, one for children. The master suite is separated into two functions—a sleeping room and a large bathing/dressing area. If Carol or Matt wakes early, each can get out of bed and get ready for the day in the dressing/bath area without disturbing his or her sleeping partner. In the children's

Know Your Lifestyle

INFORMALITY RULES at the Cozen-Bernstein house. With the noise and activity of four young children (ages 3 to 12), their friends and varied schedules, a menagerie of pets (large dog, guinea pig, bird, frogs, two aquariums full of fish), and a host of activities—everything from music lessons to homework to animal care—daily living verges on controlled chaos. Add a full working office with four employees, and the amount of traffic this house sees in a day is more than most see in a week.

The open floor plan is the key to accommodating all these people and activities, but privacy in a house like this is just as important as the social areas. Small, intimate niches are carved to create retreats. Each of the children has a place to call his or her own, and the parents have their adults-only wing, complete with Mom's well-appointed bath, which serves as her stress-relieving getaway.

Each of the children helped design his or her own room. A Midwestern barn door in this room reflects one daughter's affection for horses and slides side to side to hide either the desk on one side or the closet on the other.

wing, three bedrooms accommodate four children, who share a 7-ft. by 15-ft. bathroom with double sinks, private toilet stall, and lots of storage. A clothes chute runs directly to the laundry room below.

Paying Attention to Detail

A common criticism of modern architecture is that houses can sometimes seem cold, but that's certainly not the case here. At every turn of the design, Carol sought to warm up the house with intriguing details.

At the entry, a gently curving minimalist wall and elegant floating stairway sweep away from the foyer, drawing visitors into the space. That soft curve is repeated in the great room on the other side of the wall and again in the master bath upstairs.

Materials become décor against this clean white backdrop. Sustainable bamboo flooring throughout the lower level and upstairs hallways gives texture and warmth. A stainless-steel angle bracket introduced as a picture rail in the foyer is repeated in the fireplace mantel in the great room. Off-the-shelf maple cabinetry

Great Moves

Unlike a traditional stick-built house where everything rests under one roof, this contemporary home is designed in three sections—one wedge-shaped with a sloping roof; a long, rectangular block; and a center link connecting the two, separating public from private areas, reducing unwanted noise and traffic.

By setting priorities early, Carol maximized square footage within a tight budget. In the end, she got a 3,400-sq.-ft. house that comfortably shelters a family of seven, plus a professional office for four employees, all for $105 a sq. ft.

▪ before and after ▪

first floor

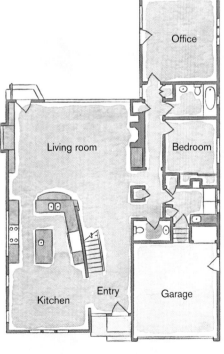

second floor

before

after

after

White marble, warm maple, and stainless steel make up the kitchen palette, a blend of warm and cold materials that allows a smooth visual flow into the adjacent areas—the dining room and great room.

warms up the library, as it does in the great room, where a wall of simple built-in cabinets stores family necessities.

Carol kept costs down by using a variety of inexpensive materials. Flooring in the studio is made up of 4x8 plywood sheets cut in half and rotated so the grain creates a checkerboard pattern. Similar ingenuity is found in the stair design, a focal point created with Plexiglas® risers, Douglas fir treads, and stainless-steel bolts.

More expensive materials are used sparingly. Carol handpicked two slabs of white marble and used every inch of them—for bathroom counters, the shower seat, and the kitchen island countertop. Wherever possible, materials are reused. In the downstairs bath, for example, a found Asian cabinet is recycled into a sink cabinet topped with a piece of marble.

A retractable built-in table makes a handy tub-side shelf for a glass of wine, a candle, or a book.

Throughout the house, small, intimate niches create spaces for retreat. This great room corner features a recessed window seat, a great private hideaway for imaginative child's play. A Dutch door to the backyard provides views and fresh air while keeping pets inside.

Visible Pegs

Although the welcome mat is always out, the Cozen-Bernstein house never seems crowded. A coat closet can fill up quickly in such an atmosphere, so Carol tried a nontraditional approach, decorating the closet door with a pattern of stainless-steel bolts for hanging coats, purses, and hats out in the open, adding to the air of informality.

Designing for Energy Efficiency

The house was built during the southern California energy crisis of 2001, and the need for energy efficiency greatly influenced the design. Because the house has no air conditioning, windows are carefully placed to take advantage of prevailing breezes. Given the mild southern California beach climate, windows and doors are left open 360 days a year, making the outdoors a vital part of the way this house lives.

Carol wanted to brighten the house naturally, relying totally on daylighting all year long without having to worry about heat gain. She incorporated direct, indirect, and diffuse light throughout the house, using different types of glazing to get the kind of light she wanted. Some glazing is clear for full-spectrum light, while other glass is sandblasted for diffuse light minus the heat.

A pattern of skylights purposefully projects shadow lines onto the two-story white wall in the foyer. These shadows spin and rotate throughout the day, creating a moving piece of art. At the entry, an 18-ft.-long translucent window illuminates the interior with diffuse light all day long. Plexiglas risers in the stairway allow diffuse ambient light to shine through, making the stairway look as though it's floating. And in all the bathrooms, a portion of the glazing is sandblasted to admit light while still maintaining privacy, thereby eliminating the need for curtains.

A row of skylights above the entry hall creates a moveable pattern of light that projects deeper into the interior as shadows lengthen. An 18-ft.-tall translucent window in the entry helps brighten the house all day long.

Light floods the entry hall, so no artificial lighting is needed. Plexiglas stair risers allow diffuse ambient light to stream through.

From Cape to Bungalow

WISH LIST

Allow for wheelchair accessibility

Accommodate visiting family

Bring more light into the house

Add a big front porch

Provide easy access to the rear yard

Pat McGuire purchased her one-story Cape in a 42-acre historic district of Asheville, N.C., fully intending to add a second story. She fell in love with the location, a planned community of 40 early-20th-century cottages, most with a botanical name. (Her property is called Seven Oaks after the huge 36-in.-diameter trees on the lawn.) Recently widowed, Pat wanted a light-filled, easily navigable house for her later years, but she also wanted enough bedrooms and baths so her large family could all visit at once and comfortably stay under one roof. A tall order for a 1,700-sq.-ft. house built in 1947.

Pat hired Samsel Architects to design the renovation, but when the roof was removed, they discovered the walls were too poorly built to support a second story. Given that Pat wanted an elevator for accessibility, and ceilings taller than the original 8 ft., it made sense to raze the structure and

as it is today

In keeping with the Arts and Crafts theme, the front door was handmade by a local craftsman and the glass insert made by a local art-glass company. Hardware here and throughout the house reflects the Arts and Crafts style.

Though this Arts and Crafts-inspired house is totally new, using the original foundation and taking care not to disturb the trees and tear up the landscape helped the structure fit into its historic neighborhood.

reframe it using the old footprint as a guide, a nod to history and to the original house.

As long as they agreed to keep the original stone foundation and not harm the large oak trees and historic stone terrace, getting permission from the Asheville Historic Resources Commission to tear down the walls wasn't difficult because the original cottage (the only one built after World War II) was nonconforming anyway. It was the property that held value in the historic landscape, not the house. Taking down the out-of-place Cape presented a welcome opportunity to design a house more in keeping with the neighborhood of Shingle style, half-timbered Tudor, and bungalow structures.

Instead of a separate family room, den, and office, Pat's library (equipped with a computer and television) fulfills all these functions.

While the Arts and Crafts theme is played down on the interior, custom moldings (especially the tapered crown molding) are indicative of the style. Ceilings are 9½ ft. high (as opposed to 8-ft.-high ceilings in the original house), giving the interior a feeling of spaciousness.

as it was ...

Using "Found" Space

Houses often have underutilized spaces that, when discovered and reconfigured for maximum utility, can satisfy the owners' requirements better and less expensively than adding on. That's what happened here. Basically, the floor plan remained the same with major living spaces in the front of the house facing the view and private areas located at the back. The program didn't call for much added space on the main living level, but rearranging interior rooms to accommodate modern, accessible living required a good deal of creativity.

Moving the basement stair freed up a lot of space, allowing for an elevator, an enlarged kitchen/breakfast room, and a front entry hall. A former bedroom became the dining room; another became the library; still another at the back of the house was reconfigured for a walk-in closet and master bathroom. Interior French doors where walls used to be open up the living room to the kitchen and back hallway. The back door moved to open onto the side yard instead of the rear yard, improving circulation in that part of the house.

Inside the front entry hall, splayed closet walls (cut back at an angle) relieve the feeling of boxiness created by 90-degree angles.

Building the master bedroom addition required a special permit since it projected from the original footprint of the house. The single-story mini-wing has a vaulted ceiling, giving it the feel of a much larger space.

Space formerly occupied by the dining room was split in two, with half used for the stairway and half a true entry hall. Orientation of the front door was changed so that instead of opening directly into the living room, it now opens into a private vestibule, creating a traditional center hall with formal spaces on each side.

Adding Out and Up

On the main level, two major additions open up the plan for spacious everyday living. The first and largest addition—a one-story, vaulted-ceiling, 14-ft. by 16-ft. master bedroom on the side of the house—adjoins the reconfigured master bath and large walk-in closet. The second addition expands the front porch in two directions, more than doubling its original size and creating an outdoor room accessible from the dining room. A couple of minor additions followed—30 sq. ft. in

The kitchen is truly the heart of the home, connected to the living room and hallway through French doors so it doesn't feel isolated and confined. Milky glass cabinet doors provide some transparency while obscuring from view what's stored on the shelves. Countertops are Corian®.

Great Moves

Aside from additions, there are three big differences between the original floor plan and the new one. Instead of being detached from daily activities, the kitchen is now the hub of the house, sharing a visual connection with the main living areas. A spacious entry vestibule provides a private welcome with coat closets flanking the front door. And French doors off the dining room provide more connection between the interior and the front porch.

Another big difference is daylighting. Arts and Crafts bungalows tend to be dark inside. This one brings in more natural light and offers more views through large expanses of windows. It also offers transparency, with interior French doors providing visual connection and shared light between the main living areas. Even on a dark day the house is filled with light.

■ before and after ■

main floor

before

after

French doors open directly from the dining room onto the large front porch, opening up the room to the outdoors and providing access to the main outdoor living area. There is no level change so a wheelchair can easily cross the threshold.

the master bath (mostly to gain a roll-in shower and a turning radius for a wheelchair) and a box bay window in the breakfast room.

Once the main-level floor plan was figured out, it wasn't difficult to configure the second story, all under-the-eaves space, keeping the house form low. The cross-gable bungalow form was a great aid in maximizing usable space. The strong gable facing the street held enough volume for two bedrooms—one in the front and one in the back. Instead of one bath (the architect's original intention), there was space for two—one for each bedroom—fitting neatly under the eaves. In the long gable, two shed dormers (one in the front and one in the back of the house) create headroom for a third bedroom over the library. Ample closets and another bath fit under the sloping roof.

All in all, there are 1,350 sq. ft. tucked under the roof—a remarkable feat.

Fitting Into the Neighborhood

Working within local guidelines, Samsel's modern bungalow is an attempt to interpret history, not resurrect it. Selection of materials, massing, and roof forms reflect those found in the neighborhood. Other features, such as the generous use of glass, are artfully integrated historical departures, small gestures that don't look out of place.

Stylistic features identifying the exterior as Arts and Crafts include its horizontal form; low overhanging rooflines; exposed eaves and brackets; heavy wood porch railing and balustrade; tapered chimney; stone piers with lattice infill; heavy textured stucco siding; and shingle siding in the upper gables and dormers. A palette of earth tones (a combination of dark trim with darker green shingles and mustard-colored stucco) reflects the style as well.

Heavy textured stucco siding painted a mustard color, the coursed shingle pattern in the upper gables and dormers, exposed brackets, and heavy porch timbers are all identifying characteristics of Arts and Crafts architecture.

Small Moves

Interior French Doors

Tall, narrow French doors separate the living room from the kitchen and rear hall. Mainly designed for sound control, the divided-light doors allow the rooms to share light while creating a visual connection so none of the rooms feels isolated and closed in. Instead of off-the-shelf French doors, these are narrow side-lights, hinged, and hung in pairs. Because they are narrow, they easily swing out of the way while still allowing the 36-in. opening necessary for wheelchair accessibility. The doors are stained, contrasting with the painted wood trim, giving a Southern plantation look to the interior.

Know Your Lifestyle

I N HER 70s, THE OWNER OF THIS HOUSE has difficulty walking and anticipates more limited mobility in the years ahead. Consequently, she designed her house for wheelchair access—with wide doorways, a barrier-free shower, doorknobs reachable from a wheelchair, and a bathroom sink with a place where a wheelchair can pull up to. In the kitchen, an undercounter cabinet is designed with a removable front panel so a wheelchair can roll up to the sink. Kitchen appliances have controls accessible from a chair.

With her bedroom, kitchen, living room, and front porch all on the main floor, everything the owner needs for everyday living is on one level. An elevator, accessible from the carport and large enough for two people, is a wonderful helper when she's unloading groceries or taking out trash. Such amenities allow her independence, so she can live alone happily without calling on her family for help.

Two shed dormers, one in the front and one in the back of the main long gable, create headroom for a third bedroom upstairs under the eaves.

In the living room, large expanses of single-pane glass topped by divided-light transoms are a modern take on the traditional Arts and Crafts window pattern.

The front window pattern—three divided-light transoms positioned over three large single sashes—sets a pattern repeated throughout, with proportions changing in the dormers. Having double-hung windows in the upper level and casement windows on the main level is a traditional Arts and Crafts feature. The use of single sashes is not.

Designing a house that fit the owner's agenda while working around the big oak trees and historic landscape was a difficult challenge, but the end result fulfills everyone's expectations. More than the one-story frame structure that preceded it, this Arts and Crafts bungalow looks as if it has always been a part of this historic neighborhood.

A two-person elevator designed for wheelchair accessibility is located off the carport and ascends to the main living area.

A-Frame
Overhaul

WISH LIST

Open up the house

Provide space for dinner parties

Bring in natural light

Use lots of light-colored wood

Improve access to private front garden

Built in 1962, this 1,200-sq.-ft. A-frame was typical for its era—a timber frame built on stilts on a steep hillside in an unincorporated area five miles from San Francisco and the Golden Gate Bridge. Although a sliver of a city view can be seen from the driveway, the main view from the house is due south, overlooking Homestead Valley, a heavily wooded community.

Like many West Coast hillside A-frames, the front door opens onto the uppermost level at the peak—a tiny entry hall with mezzanine overlooking the main living area, which is reached by a central stair. A late 1980s remodeling added a stabilizing perimeter foundation and a third lower level, 800 sq. ft. farther down the hillside, containing two bedrooms, one and a half baths, a laundry, storage, and a full-length deck.

By the time Catherine Fowler and Jim Karavias found the house in the late 1990s, it combined the worst of 1960s and

The main level of the house is one big open space—with entry/mezzanine above and kitchen, living, dining, and den below. An open-riser central stair with transparent railings connects the two levels, permitting long views.

The living room wall was bumped out 1 ft. to house a fireplace insert. An exposed metal chimney, routed up the side of the house, pops through the roof a few feet from its peak.

'70s style. Interiors were dark and cavelike, with exposed posts and beams covered with heavy-handed dark stain, orange shag buried under a layer of cheap beige carpeting, and heavy volcanic rock on the fireplace facing. Cathy, who had moved to the Bay Area from a tiny, dark apartment in New York, wanted a comfortable, bright, light-filled house with expansive views of the outdoors. Jim concurred, and their friend, designer Mark Wilson, assured them that the house held such possibilities.

Opening Up Walls and Ceilings

Initially, the couple wanted to upgrade the quality of the house by increasing the size of the bathroom and kitchen, changing some windows, and freshening up finishes. They soon realized that to do the job properly within budget meant they would have to put their money into quality finishes and eliminate the bathroom remodel. The final agenda called for retaining the original structure but tearing down interior walls and part of the kitchen ceiling to open up the plan.

The den (formerly the dining room) is tucked away behind the open-riser central stair. Although separate from the main living area, the two rooms are visibly connected because the transparent railings allow a see-through view from one space to the other.

The fireplace wall in the living room received special treatment, with a 4x4 cherry mantel extended a couple of inches out from the wall and affixed with industrial-looking brackets. The wall is heavy-textured stucco painted a pale gray that pulls out the lighter tones in the green limestone facing of the fireplace.

Originally, the living room was an oversized space with a tin can fireplace insert covered with lava rock on the short wall. In reworking the floor plan, the living room was split in two with half given to a new dining room, a move that made the living room a more intimate space. The fireplace was relocated into the now-smaller living area, not a difficult change since a 1-ft. bumpout was built to house a more efficient fireplace insert and a metal chimney routed up the side of the house.

The kitchen, a tiny linoleum and plywood galley enclosed by four walls and a low ceiling, required a more complex fix. Here, part of the ceiling was removed and a mini-cathedral ceiling built with a big

as it was ...

Great Moves

Initially, the living room was an oversized space. In reworking the floor plan, the existing dining room (which was too small for a dining table anyway) became a den/music room, and the oversized living room was split in half, with half given to the new dining room. In the kitchen, an L-shaped wall was removed to make one great room—a kitchen/dining/ living heart of the home. The kitchen inched 35 sq. ft. into the new dining area. Upstairs, a closet was deepened and the ceiling lowered to create a more protective entry with expansive views to the open living area below, helping first-time visitors orient themselves in the house more quickly.

■ before and after ■

main floor

before

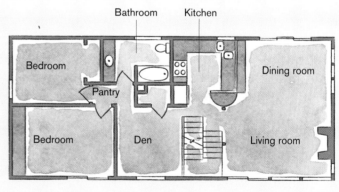

after

entry level

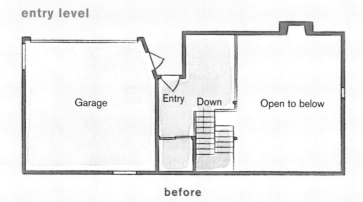

before

after

Built-in Buffet

Cathy and Jim didn't want a separate kitchen where the cook is isolated from family or dinner guests. They enjoy entertaining, so an open kitchen/dining area was at the top of their wish list. A wall separating the two rooms was removed and an 8½-ft.-long peninsula built with a hardworking limestone counter on the kitchen side and a lower wood buffet counter, with lots of storage underneath, on the dining room side. A 6-in.-tall raised counter separates the two, shielding guests from kitchen messes. A half-circle eating bar with two stools at the end of the peninsula is used to serve appetizers or as additional workspace where guests can take part in meal preparation. As a finishing touch, a 2x4 piece of cherry extends 4-in. over the buffet, creating additional design interest.

skylight in the roof, allowing the kitchen to share volume and light with the entry above. The kitchen's most peculiar feature, a little pickup window (a 6-ft. by 1½-ft. slit in the wall, looking as though it was designed for a short-order cook), definitely had to go. This interior L-shaped wall was removed, opening up the kitchen to living and dining areas and making one great room.

Reworking the Entry

Reworking the dark, uninviting entry at the peak of the vaulted ceiling made a big difference in the first impression visitors get of the house. Before, the ceiling was uncomfortably high, and the sharp fall of the roof made head height too low for much of the space to be usable. Removing a portion of the floor over the kitchen (to open up views) further reduced floor space, as did moving an interior wall to the center to deepen the coat closet and give it more height. With these changes, the resulting entry contains only 230 sq. ft. of usable floor space.

Industrial fittings (threaded rod, steel plate, and bolts) create a mount and an arm at the kitchen counter, a surprising detail that contrasts with the otherwise neat and polished interior.

Once a drab, uncomfortable space, the entry is now a welcoming introduction to the house, with its spot-lit niches, big roof window, and transparent balcony rail. A sofa table offers a spot to drop off keys, mail, and packages.

The original tongue-and-groove knotty pine ceiling was retained, and some of the dark-stained posts and beams were encased in drywall and painted white for a bright, clean look.

The solution called for dropping a flat, 8-ft. soffit over the entry, creating a more comfortably proportioned space. A dark wood entry door was replaced with a light wood door with a window in it for transparency. Niches were built into the wall and spot-lit to display pieces of the couple's pottery collection. The heavy, dark balcony rail was replaced with a modern design of steel cable strung between clean-lined cherry wood posts.

Walking in the front door, the owners (and guests) now get a sense of protection created by the lowered ceiling and are greeted with quality materials, such as the multicolored Brazilian slate floor.

The transparent mezzanine stair rail allows a preview of the living area below, making the layout of the house instantly intelligible. And the open-riser central stair invites visitors down, drawing them toward the space and the light.

Creating a Bright, Clean Look

Selected posts and beams of the dark-stained timber frame were encased in drywall and painted white, yielding a clean-lined bright skeleton supporting all rooms of the house. In a single move, the heavy, dim interior began to feel lighter. The introduction of light wood throughout the house—cherry cabinets in the kitchen, cherry stair casing and maple treads, a tongue-and-groove knotty pine ceiling, and light maple floor—helped remove all traces of the dark interior.

The shingled A-frame is built on stilts on a steeply sloping hillside among a stand of redwood trees, with wraparound decks at two levels offering panoramic views of Homestead Valley.

Steel cable wire strung between cherry wood posts gives a clean, contemporary look, replacing dark and heavy wood railings that blocked the light.

THE SEVEN

Know Your Property

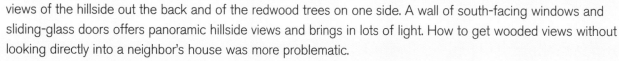

THE STEEP HILLSIDE SITE was one of the real challenges of this house. With neighbors close on both sides, a 20-ft. setback from the street, and nowhere to build down the hill, all changes had to take place inside the existing structure.

Cathy and Jim wanted a light-filled house with expansive views of the hillside out the back and of the redwood trees on one side. A wall of south-facing windows and sliding-glass doors offers panoramic hillside views and brings in lots of light. How to get wooded views without looking directly into a neighbor's house was more problematic.

Designer Mark Wilson solved the dilemma by adding a group of three clerestory windows just above head height on the east wall of the dining room, allowing light and ventilation while still giving privacy. In the living room, on one side of the fireplace, he stacked five small clerestory windows vertically to frame views into the trees. On the other side of the fireplace, 10 ft. and 15 ft. up in the peak of the house, he placed two square clerestory windows that highlight the top of the redwood tree and are the first thing a visitor sees from the entrance.

Even private parts of the house have panoramic views and a good indoor/outdoor connection. The entire south-facing wall of the A-frame overlooking the valley opens onto a wraparound deck through expansive windows and sliding-glass doors.

A private shade garden is tucked into the front of the house beneath the drive-way, where it is shielded from the wind.

A good indoor-outdoor connection helps extend views, making the house feel bigger. Because the house sits on a steep slope, it does not have a usable yard, but tiered wraparound decks overlooking the hillside more than make up for the lack of space at ground level. Big sliding-glass doors trimmed in wood open off the living room, den, and bedroom, offering panoramic views from inside the house as well as from the sunny back deck. Matching triple sliding doors added to the dining area (where the fireplace once stood) connect it with a sheltered front garden.

The result is a complete transformation. What was once a dark, claustrophobic house is now a lively, bright environment flooded with natural light all day long, blessed with expansive views and an open plan under a 23-ft.-high vaulted ceiling.

Farmhouse
Revisited

After scouring the Seattle region for several years, the owners of this house found the perfect place to transplant their family from the suburbs and start an organic berry farm—almost perfect, that is. The Whidbey Island property had so much going for it: a pleasant community; 40 acres of rich, picturesque farmland; a home overlooking the Olympic Mountains and the nearby Puget Sound ship canal. The problems? The 1960s ranch house was dark, dated, and, with just two bedrooms, far too small for a family of four. Besides, it was not for sale.

Undeterred, the Seattle dwellers, who are former Midwesterners with farming roots, arranged to meet the elderly couple who owned the farm. At the meeting, everybody felt an instant bond. When the couple retired three years later, they happily sold the property to their new friends.

as it is today

The bay window and seating nook pull light into the kitchen. To increase food preparation space, architect Mitch Yockey made the counters an extra-deep 30 in.; the maple-faced cabinets under them are standard, 24-in.-deep units set 6 in. off the wall. Because the homeowners are not tall, the island is 2 in. lower than standard.

The cozy sitting area in the master bedroom is warmed by a quaint but efficient furnace-rated gas stove.

Although filled with potential, the low-slung farmhouse needed work. It sat on a hilltop and angled toward the mountain and water vistas but managed to ignore the views. Even the kitchen, which occupied the southwesterly corner with the best vantage point, had only two skimpy windows. The living space on the 1,525-sq.-ft. main floor was reasonable in size but chopped up by jogs and turns, confining walls, and a huge masonry enclosure surrounding a cast-iron woodstove. The owners were eager to create a sunny, open interior that would embrace the breathtaking surroundings.

They also needed more space, both for their family and for visiting relatives who would come often and stay for extended periods. One day when repairing the old roof, the owners discovered that the views were even better from higher up. That discovery, plus their goal of adding space without adding sprawl, drove the decision to stack most of the new space on top of the existing house.

Large windows in the master bedroom celebrate the view. Intersecting ceiling planes subtly define spaces in the room; a bend in the wall forms a niche for the balcony.

The fireplace bumpout in the living room extends down to the walkout basement, where a compact wood-burning stove warms a corner of the new media room. At the other end of the 640-sq.-ft. basement are an extra bath and a root cellar.

Making Small Add-Ons Count

In the remodeled house, the master bedroom suite and private balcony occupy the western half of the 1,165-sq.-ft. second story, facing the most beautiful views. The children's bedrooms and bath fill the rest of the new floor. The first-floor bedroom area became a guest suite, and the lower-level family room was reshaped as a media room/spill-over guest quarters.

Aside from the second floor, architect Mitch Yockey added only 145 sq. ft. to the house, but those few feet have a dramatic impact. Yockey removed interior walls and the masonry enclosure to turn the kitchen-dining-living area into a casual, integrated living space. With two small kitchen additions—an eating nook and a bay

Great Moves

The main-floor living areas were arranged well, but jutting walls, a massive woodstove enclosure, and unnecessary jogs and turns chopped up the space and made rooms feel cramped. By removing those obstructions, architect Mitch Yockey created an open, less confined interior that looks brighter, feels bigger, and is more versatile. The wall at the basement stairs remains but has been shortened to expand the view between entry and living room.

■ before and after ■

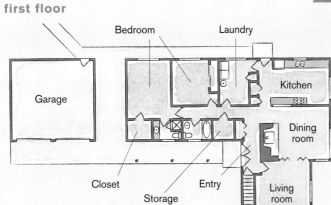

first floor

Bedroom
Laundry
Garage
Kitchen
Closet
Dining room
Storage
Entry
Living room

before

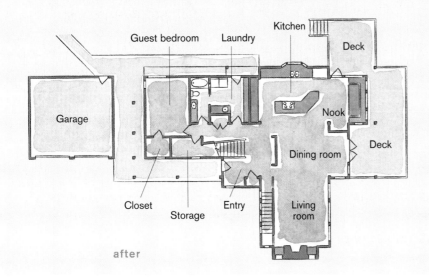

Guest bedroom
Laundry
Kitchen
Deck
Garage
Nook
Deck
Closet
Storage
Entry
Dining room
Living room

after

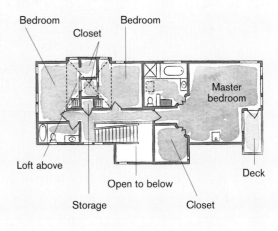

second floor

Bedroom
Closet
Bedroom
Master bedroom
Loft above
Deck
Open to below
Closet
Storage

after

window—he was able to open the kitchen to sunlight and views that penetrate the entire living area.

In addition to removing partition walls, Yockey eliminated jogs in the perimeter walls to create a clean, simple rectangle surrounding the living area. A third little bumpout, this one in the living room, carves out space for a cozy fireplace and inset cabinets that neither disrupt the smooth perimeter nor take up floor area. The only other addition on the main floor is an entryway. Originally the front door opened into the fireplace wall; now the house has an entry foyer that greets visitors with views through the living area and French doors to the deck and the mountains beyond.

Lofty ceilings and big windows enhance the feeling of openness in the house. A palette of light wood tones and white walls creates a sunny aspect, even on gray days. To soften the tones and make the space feel warm and friendly, Yockey used wide Douglas fir flooring strips and roughsawn fir posts and beams. Reinforcing that cordial spirit, a big, curved kitchen island invites everyone into the farm kitchen. There's room for a gang to sit at the curved counter or help with the cooking.

The new second floor was stacked directly over the first floor, giving the house a clean, rectangular shape. The second-story pop-out, sheathed in corrugated metal, delivers the message that something new and different is going on.

Wide and gracious at the base, the main stairway creates a clever optical illusion by narrowing as it rises. Light filters through the upstairs balusters to brighten the way. Those tiny portholes in the upstairs wall are lookouts from the kids' loft.

A ladder from each child's bedroom (top left and left) rises to a shared loft that fills surplus space over the kids' closets. The 8-ft. by 10-ft. room has three square exterior windows and two that overlook the main stairway; floor-to-ceiling rails keep the loft open but safe.

Transparent Railing

Not wanting to look at their scenic surroundings through the pickets of a deck railing, the homeowners came up with the alternative of using glass panels. They were sold on the idea when their builder said it would be less expensive to insert the panels than to install dozens of pickets. The tempered-glass sheets are supported by cedar posts about 4 ft. apart. Virtually maintenance free, the panels fog up in the morning mist, then become clean and clear. Unlike plastic, the glass will not scratch or yellow.

Yockey had fun with the main staircase: He made the treads shorter as they approach the second floor, creating a forced perspective. The homeowners enjoy the witty design and say the stairs are a guaranteed conversation starter. Yockey applied more sleight of hand upstairs, where angled entries from the master bedroom to the master bath and closet effectively expand the bedroom. The crowning touch upstairs is the lookout loft over the kids' closets. The kids share the loft, which is accessible from a ladder in each child's bedroom.

Cultivating a Farmhouse Feel

To respect its rural surroundings, the owners wanted the exterior of the house to resemble an old-time farm building. Yockey used the "language" of farm structures—typical shapes, colors, and materials—to wrap the modernized home in a traditional skin. Plain walls, minimal trim, and steep rooflines evoke the farmhouse feel. So do the barn-red paint that covers most of the house and the simple, white window frames.

Everybody knows the archetypal farm scene where the house and outbuildings cluster at the end of a long, dirt road. Yockey played with that classic image to make the much-enlarged house look less bulky. Sheathed in industrial corrugated metal, not unlike silo siding, all the bumpouts stand apart visually from the main walls.

The house has rhythm and diversity, combining old and new. Traditional features such as red paint, spare trim, and pertly pitched and shed roofs mix comfortably with shiny, industrial-look smokestacks and bands of square triplet windows.

THE SEVEN

Know Your Property

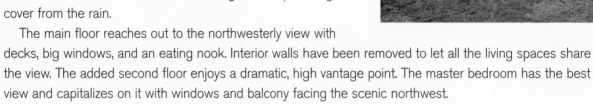

PERCHED ON A HILL facing mountains and Puget Sound, the Whidbey Island house has a view that won't quit—and a Washington climate of moderate temperatures and frequent, misty rains that won't quit either. Yockey's design opens the house to the view and available natural light, while providing cover from the rain.

The main floor reaches out to the northwesterly view with decks, big windows, and an eating nook. Interior walls have been removed to let all the living spaces share the view. The added second floor enjoys a dramatic, high vantage point. The master bedroom has the best view and capitalizes on it with windows and balcony facing the scenic northwest.

Deep roof overhangs lend afternoon shade and shelter the deck from wind-blown rain, making it usable for cookouts year-round. Another overhanging roof protects the walkway between the garage and entry.

Corrugated metal siding, shed roofs, and rustic wood posts tag the entry bumpout as an addition but look at home on a farm. The deep roof overhang shelters the entry.

as it was ...

The master bathroom tub surround doubles as a seating ledge in the shower, and a skylight partners with the window to bring in lots of light. Radiant in-floor heating warms the slate tile floor; the same system heats the entry, kitchen, and mudroom.

Shed roofs of various lengths disguise additions on the entry façade as annexes. Coming up the long driveway, visitors see a residence that blends subtle contemporary accents with the flavor and appeal of a pristine house nestled against assorted farm buildings.

Environmentally Friendly Features

True to their calling as organic farmers, the homeowners were determined to use environmentally friendly materials in their house. A recycling opportunity emerged early on, when three Douglas fir trees that had been topped years earlier and were growing dangerously close to the house had to be cut down. The homeowners had the lumber milled and used the wood from those large trees as posts and beams inside and outside the house.

The fir flooring strips came from a Seattle salvage company, which preserved beams from old warehouses and cut them into flooring pieces. The floors and other exposed fir elements—doors, trim, posts, and beams—are finished with natural oil and wax. Linoleum, made of cork and linseed oil, makes a homey, natural kitchen floor well suited to a country house. Slate tile in the mudroom and bath is hardy and handsome. Soapstone kitchen counters look beautiful now and will acquire a rich patina over time.

As it comes into view from the driveway, the house looks like a cluster of farm buildings.

Rescuing a
Burned-Out Shell

WISH LIST

Accommodate all necessary living spaces on the first floor

Include two separate studies

Provide a bright, naturally lit interior

Incorporate a rental unit

After their children left home, Bill and Ruth Hsiao entered what Bill describes as a "hollow phase." Their large Victorian home with its high-ceilinged rooms and dark corners felt lonely and wasteful. They decided to sell the home and return to the congenial neighborhood of their graduate school days, near the Charles River in Cambridge, Mass., a five-minute walk from Harvard Square.

Houses in this desirable neighborhood (near walking trails, bicycle paths, and boat races) don't often come up for sale, but the Hsiaos found one before it hit the market—a plain, two-story Second Empire three-plex built around 1880 in a modest neighborhood of laborers' houses designed for carpenters, gardeners, plumbers, and others who serviced the big houses one block over. Originally, the 2,400-sq.-ft. structure housed three families, with each family having two lower-floor rooms and two second-story rooms.

This angled bay window, and another just like it on the other side of the fireplace wall, adds depth and transparency, brightening the interior with natural light while alleviating the claustrophobia of boxy rooms.

When the Hsiaos purchased the derelict property, it was ugly by any stretch of the imagination. Asbestos shingles covered up original clapboard siding, and a fire had left the interior severely water damaged—with plaster falling off the walls, moldy furniture, and 2x4s rotting by the day. It would take a complete gutting to save it, but the house (in a historic district) was worth it. Bill and Ruth drew up a wish list (which included the desire for a rental unit) and hired architect Jeremiah Eck to design the renovation.

Breaking Out of the Box

Originally, the house was a flat-roofed rectangle. To satisfy the Hsiaos' desire for light-filled interiors and a feeling of spaciousness (not a series of boxy rooms), it was necessary to break out of the box.

Building even tiny additions proved problematic, as zoning laws permitted only a small amount of new square footage. With their neighbors' support, the Hsiaos received a variance to make a few

Several bumpouts and boxed-out windows keep the exterior façade from appearing flat while adding depth and dimension to interior rooms.

The front portico is actually the renter's entrance leading up to the second story. It repeats the arch-shape motif found elsewhere in the house and features historic details such as wide moldings, dentils, and a wrought-iron cornice rail.

A peninsula separates the kitchen from the dining room, providing countertop eating space. Glass cabinet doors above the peninsula increase transparency from the front of the house to the back.

modest changes, the most drastic being the addition of a partial third floor and a new gambrel roof with a gable popping out of the top. Under this new "hat," several small additions open up interior rooms while giving depth and dimension to the otherwise flat façade.

Added features breaking out of the boxy, rectangular form include two 3-ft.-deep angled bays filled with floor-to-ceiling windows at the rear of the house; an exposed fireplace chimney between the bays, as well as a little deck leading to the backyard; two second-story balconies above the bays; a boxed-out window over the kitchen sink and another in the guest bedroom on the opposite side of the house; a side entry porch with an arched roof and little stair; and an elaborately detailed front portico including a boxed-out window with a pediment roof, adding dimension to the front façade.

The compact U-shaped kitchen contains cherry panel cabinetry with transparent glass doors and black marble countertops—a rich, harmonious, and simple palette.

Making Space

Great space is more than just a good two-dimensional floor plan; it's also about the three-dimensional quality created by varying ceiling heights. Architect Jeremiah Eck attended to both when designing a new plan that eked out as much space as possible within the existing footprint.

Originally, this three-plex was divided into thirds side to side with stairs bisecting the structure. In this case, purchasing a burned-out shell was a blessing because the plan could be totally reshaped without the tedious chore of working around existing features.

While the house presents a formal streetside façade with a historic character, the rear is more relaxed, with a wealth of windows and bumpouts overlooking a shady patio.

A window-filled arch over the main entry at the side of the house repeats the arch shape found over the front entry and in clerestory windows at the roof's peak.

Cherry wood cabinetry creates a rich focal point against a pale backdrop of white walls and fir flooring. Contoured shelves in the fireplace wall repeat the reverse curve found in the angled bumpout bays on either side.

THE SEVEN

Know Your Place

THIS HOUSE sits in a dense neighborhood of similarly styled houses, each built around the turn of the last century. Though it originally did not have a gambrel roof, the distinctive hipped roof style is usually found on Second Empire houses and is commonly found in Cambridge, so giving this transformed dwelling a gambrel roof (permitting third-floor living space) was a natural.

Like its neighbors, the house is banded into distinct thirds—a brick base, a clapboard middle, and a shingled "hat." Such banding gives it a horizontal quality that makes it feel lower than its two-and-a-half story height.

The historical character of the neighborhood is also expressed in elaborate exterior detailing—multipaned windows, dentils along the roof's edge, a symmetrical façade with centered entry, a regular rhythm of windows, and paired windows above the porch. Subtle variations express a modern quality, especially the extra-wide clapboards that help give the tall house a horizontal appearance. Such subtle deviation makes the house unique, while still allowing it to fit unobtrusively into the streetscape.

Where New Meets Old

Zoning restrictions limited additions to bay windows, rear decks, an exposed chimney, an arched side entrance, and a boxed-out pedimented front window—each butting up against the flat façade of the old house. The owners received a variance allowing them to add a partial third floor under a new gambrel roof, which contains a pop-up gable in the center filled with skylights and clerestory windows. Each addition has a contemporary quality, especially the side entrance with its arched roof.

A wall at the far end of the 35-ft.-long living room/sitting room is lined with bookshelves and a built-in desk for quiet reading, writing letters, and paying bills.

One of the ways Eck achieved a luxurious use of space was to place the main entrance on the side of the house, thereby gaining the full width of the footprint instead of having a hallway down the middle. The Hsiaos have the entire first floor. The second level is split down the middle side to side, with the Hsiaos' studies in the back and rental space in the front. The new third floor, tucked into added space in the gambrel roof, is also shared—half for a cathedral ceiling in each study and half for a large room and bath for the renter.

Carving out the house in this manner permitted the Hsiaos to have all necessary living spaces on the first level and gave them lots of height as well, so rooms feel spacious. The main stair the Hsiaos use to access the second floor goes all the way up to the window-filled pop-up on the roof. Even the rental unit has an arched clerestory window and cathedral ceiling.

A wall of windows at the rear of the house extends to the second floor, where natural light brightens the two studies. A door in each study leads to a balcony deck, breaking out of the rectangular house form while providing a good indoor/outdoor connection.

Cathedral ceilings in each of the second-floor studies add volume, making the small spaces feel bigger and creating room for a loft.

Points of Focus

Focus is an important element of successful design: It's the exclamation point, the icing on the cake. If everything is the same, a structure has no point of interest. The interior of this house has two main focal points—the fireplace wall shared by the living room and sitting room, and the stairwell rising a dramatic two-and-a-half stories to the peak of the roof. Both are visible from the front entry, giving the first-time visitor a sense of delight in what was previously a dark, drab interior.

The gently curved fireplace wall, flanked by two angled bays filled with floor-to-ceiling windows, is the dominant focal point, drawing visitors from the entry into the most public room in the house. Built of cherry wood with black slate accents, the contemporary wall design

Great Moves

In order for the house to suit them in their later years, the owners wanted to accommodate all living spaces on the first floor, including bedroom, bathroom, and walk-in closets. With two spacious studies on the second floor—one for him and one for her—the house also fits the way the couple works. They can each go into their own separate study, close the door, and be in their own world.

Entertaining friends is also an important part of their lives. The couple wanted two living areas—one for entertaining (the living room) and a quieter sitting room for reading, listening to music, and watching television. Ruth wanted a kitchen open to the dining area so the cook wouldn't be isolated during parties. All this is integrated into an open plan so the main living areas aren't separated and contained.

before and after

first floor

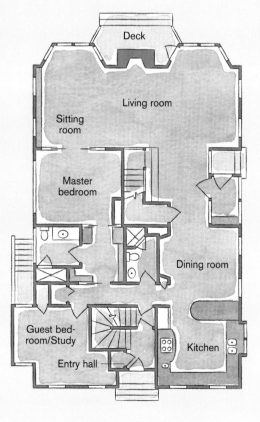

Deck

Living room

Sitting room

Master bedroom

Dining room

Guest bedroom/Study

Entry hall

Kitchen

after

second floor

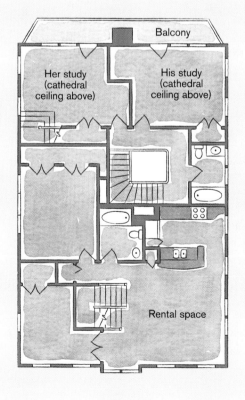

Balcony

Her study (cathedral ceiling above)

His study (cathedral ceiling above)

Rental space

after

A dramatic curving stairwell inside the foyer rises 36 ft., bringing natural light from rooftop skylights deep into the interior of all three levels.

The curved fireplace wall that straddles the divide between living room and sitting room is the most contemporary element in the 125-year-old house. Hearth, mantel, and countertops are black slate; the wood is cherry.

features contoured bookshelves on either side of the fireplace, echoing the reverse curve of the bumpout bays.

The main stairwell curves and switches back along its 36-ft. rise to the rooftop, creating a funnel of light cascading from skylights and clerestory windows punched into the pop-up gable in the center of the roof. Both of these focal points beckon you forward, making you curious about what lies ahead, and give the house a unique quality not found in cookie-cutter floor plans.

A pop-up gable in the center of the new gambrel roof contains three skylights and two arched clerestory windows that illuminate the stairwell.

Picture

Perfect Porch

Open up a boxy house

Create an outdoorsy summer gathering place

Provide a seamless match with the existing house

As soon as the weather turns warm in May, David Fredrickson and his wife, Jana Martin, grab their dinner plates and make a beeline for the screen porch. Not until mid-September do they eat another meal in the dining room. Whether the weather is warm or cool, rainy or dry, they like to be out on the porch. When company comes, the porch is where they gather.

David and Jana's enthusiasm for the porch is no surprise. For seven years, they and their two children lived in their small Tudor-style house before it had a porch, feeling as if they were sealed in a shoebox. Both David and Jana love the outdoors, but the St. Paul, Minn., house offered limited access to it. David had planted a sea of flowers in the back-yard, which nobody could really see. The closest thing to a porch was the tiny sunroom, and that had been usurped by their daughter as a place to practice the cello.

Filled with light and fresh air, trimmed in the same dusty green as the exterior, and finished with textured paint to look like the stucco siding, the porch feels like an outdoor space.

David and Jana were eager to have a room that immersed them in the outdoors, but they didn't want it to look merely tacked on. Architect Robert Gerloff designed an addition that has all the best qualities of a porch but looks integral to the house.

Extending Outdoors, Expanding Indoors

With a ceiling open to the rafters and large screened windows on four sides, the 12-ft. by 16-ft. porch is as outdoorsy as can be. Natural, Douglas fir ceiling boards and trusses evoke the charm of a cabin in the woods. The hardy, weather-resistant concrete flooring is an outdoor standard. Textured, ivory walls and muted green trim express the outdoors in a more subtle way by matching the exterior of the house.

The porch addition is such a good match for the main house that it looks original—almost. The large screen openings mimic the windows in pattern but are big and bountiful to drink in the fresh air.

THE SEVEN

Know Your Structure

IN A ROOM with a full cathedral ceiling, the roof-support system is exposed. It needs to be engineered to carry the load, but there's no reason not to treat it as a design asset as well.

A system of supporting triangular trusses is the best stylistic fit for a Tudor house. One advantage of trusses is that the timbers can be relatively slender without reducing the strength of the triangular forms. Architect Robert Gerloff took advantage of that to create a web of trim Douglas fir timbers well proportioned for the size of the room. He gave some of the timbers a graceful curve, which also conforms to Tudor practice.

Instead of mortising the timbers together, Gerloff designed beautiful steel gusset plates to connect them. His abstract, fluid design—suggesting flowers, flames, or sun rays—comes in three variations to fit different joints. Painted brownish red, the metal fasteners blend with the floor and raise the artistic level of the room sky high.

first floor

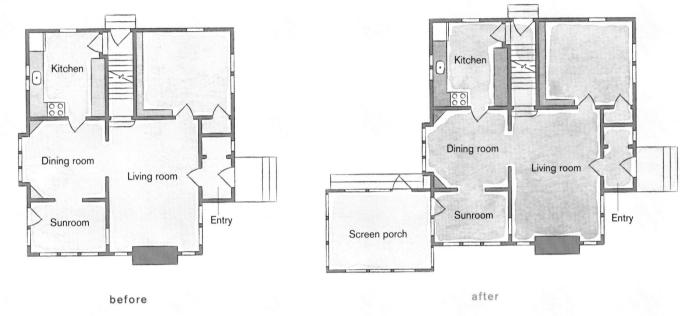

before

after

as it was ...

The addition projects just 4 ft. beyond the side of the main house, honoring the building's trim proportions while giving the porch extra breathing room. The window on the narrow wall provides views of big, old oak trees; a deep roof overhang shields it from the sun and rain.

Light and fresh air penetrate the room from morning to night, and a ceiling fan keeps the breezes flowing. To protect the room from too much sun, the top half of the west-facing end wall is solid, punctuated only by a high, operable window that ventilates the room and channels a shaft of light to the center of the space.

The porch thrusts out from the back of house with long sides exposed, maximizing its connection to the yard. Where it meets the existing house it forms a sheltered ell. The screen door opens to this inviting corner, which is currently used for a garden but could also accommodate a patio someday. Outside the door, a band of steps as wide as the addition works as extra seating for outdoor gatherings or as a ledge to display potted plants.

Just as the porch extends the house outward, it expands the living area inside. It is attached to the sunroom, incorporating that formerly dead-end space into a dynamic area where the family can

The porch makes the house live bigger by adding space, light, and a long view through the sunroom and living room. To bring in light but conserve wall space for furniture, Gerloff used a window and a single French door between the porch and sunroom rather than double doors.

Concrete Like Tile

A few tricks turned the concrete floor into a stunning, terrazzo tile look-alike. Deep red coloring was added to the concrete mix to permeate the flooring with a warm earth tone. Then control joints were scored in a pattern resembling large tiles. When the dyed floor came out looking less than perfect, the builder ground it down and burnished it. The process exposed a striking surface of tiny stones floating in deep red concrete.

Another way to spruce up concrete flooring is to stain it. Sprayed-on dye is absorbed by the lime in the concrete mix. Once the residue is scrubbed off, the floor displays the variegated coloration of marble.

Oriented at a right angle to the house, the porch connects to the main structure without adding to its bulk. David is planting new gardens that will be visible from all sides of the room.

feel connected while sitting in different rooms. Where the sunroom meets the porch, Gerloff added a French door next to an existing window. At the other end of the sunroom he replaced a door with a window, retaining the light but giving the room a stronger sense of enclosure. Now light and views flow from garden to porch to sunroom and through to the front of the house.

An Exterior That Matches Perfectly

In contrast to the flimsy-looking porch additions that are typically slapped on, David and Jana's porch really belongs. It is a true extension of the house, reflecting every detail of the Tudor exterior. The stucco and trim match. The porch roof matches the house's roof in pitch, overhang, material, and color. The windows and screens align, and the screens repeat the pattern of the existing windows. Only the generous size of the screens reveals that the addition, which looks so much like the house, lives so much like the outdoors.

Cottage
Fixer-Upper

- Create an accessible, casual cottage
- Provide open living space
- Add three bedrooms and two baths on new second floor
- Stay within a modest budget

Rod Wright's family has lived on Jamestown Island in Narragansett Bay, R. I., for six generations, so Rod always had a hunch he'd settle there one day. After he met and married Natalie Waters, the young Boston-based professional couple spent holidays and weekends touring the island looking for property for sale. When they found this tiny white summer cottage, built shortly after 1900, they instantly knew it was the place for them. They fell in love with its authenticity, its lack of pretension, the romance of its small, intimate rooms . . . and the low price tag.

On the downside, the fixer-upper needed a tremendous amount of work just to make it habitable—the roof leaked, the furnace needed replacing, and a family of skunks lived in the crawl space under the house.

To keep the cottage scale intact, new shed dormers on the rear were designed to look like two separate elements—two 8-ft. sections with a 4-ft. recessed section in the middle.

The upstairs master bedroom has plenty of headroom thanks to a steep roof pitch and 7-ft.-high walls in the shed dormer.

Rob and Natalie soon realized they had little idea how to transform the decrepit structure into the house of their dreams. The challenge was to renovate the old cottage but keep the original integrity intact, to double the size but not overwhelm the original structure, and to do it all on a tight budget. They hired architect Ron DiMauro, who specializes in period design, to bring their vision to life.

Adding Up

When DiMauro first saw the 1,100-sq.-ft. cottage, he realized everything needed updating. Electrical and plumbing systems were not compliant with code; the staircase was too steep and unsafe; floor joists and the center carrying beam were rotted; and the roof leaked. The unfinished attic was suitable for storage, but that was all. And there was no basement, only a rudimentary foundation resting on cedar posts.

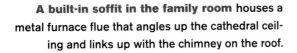

A built-in soffit in the family room houses a metal furnace flue that angles up the cathedral ceiling and links up with the chimney on the roof.

The master suite is nestled under the roof of two separate shed dormers (the sleeping room in the back, the bathroom in the front), but it has the headroom of a full second story.

Beadboard Doors

All-new interior doors (like this slanted closet door in the master bath) are easy to build out of inexpensive 1x6x¾-in. tongue-and-groove beadboard reinforced with a Z back. Beadboard, with its vertical lines and shadows, is reminiscent of old-fashioned kitchen pantries, where it was used to protect the walls. Given that history, beadboard conjures up warmth and charm, two distinct traits of cottage style. In this master bath, it's also used in a partial wall to help shield the clawfoot tub.

Every useable square inch was eked out of the second floor, including a 9-ft. by 10-ft. space for a playroom tucked into the side gable over the kitchen.

To keep the intimate scale and proportion of the single-story cottage, DiMauro decided to add roof dormers to gain headroom in the attic for the additional bedrooms and baths Rod and Natalie wanted. To add up safely, the entire structure had to be strengthened with a new foundation. So, a big trench was dug underneath the house and a new 7-ft. concrete foundation poured to add a full basement in which to store utilities. The old roof was torn off and replaced with a steeper pitched roof, then one shed dormer was built in the front and another in the rear, both inset a few feet from the sides of the house so the exterior shape appears similar to the original.

To keep the cottage scale intact, each dormer is designed to look like two separate elements—an 8-ft. section on the left (containing three double-hung windows), an 8-ft. section on the right (again with three double-hung windows), and a 4-ft. section recessed 8 in. in the middle—a fool-the-eye trick that makes you think there are two small dormers on each side instead of one big one. Where there was no habitable space at all, there are now three bedrooms, two baths, and a 9-ft. by 10-ft. playroom.

The 12-ft. by 12-ft. dining room, formerly a bedroom, is now part of the open plan. Stairs are typical cottage-style with a white newel post, square white balusters, white risers, red oak treads, and a natural red oak handrail. Flooring is original red oak.

Open Yet Intimate Living Space

A lot of walls came down on the main level, creating interior space for the stairs and more natural traffic flow. Living spaces, which were small and separated by walls, are now arranged in an open L, with the family room and living room flanking the kitchen. Thirty-six-inch-high kneewalls provide physical separation yet maintain visibility so someone standing in the kitchen can keep an eye on children playing in the family room as well as feel a part of adult activities taking place in the living room.

Because the family room doesn't have habitable space above it, a cathedral ceiling adds volume, making the 13-ft. by 16-ft. space feel considerably bigger. In the living room, original accordion French doors were retrofitted and kept for the light and views and for the simple charm of a wall of windows with immediate outdoor access.

A partial wall separates the breakfast and living rooms yet keeps the spaces visibly open to each other, maintaining the intimacy of a cottage without hindering the open plan. The 14-in.-thick wall provides cookbook storage on the kitchen side.

Great Moves

Before renovation, the old layout of small rooms with many doorways and lots of wasted circulation space cried out to be opened up and modernized. The agenda called for removing and changing walls, adding windows, and rerouting the staircase.

Relocating the stair solved myriad problems, creating space for an open kitchen/dining area downstairs; permitting traffic to arrive in the center of the second floor; and making it possible to access two bedrooms and a bath off a small upstairs hall.

before and after

first floor

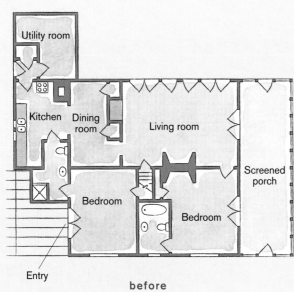

Utility room

Kitchen

Dining room

Living room

Screened porch

Bedroom

Bedroom

Entry

before

Family room

Kitchen

Breakfast area

Living room

Entry

Screened porch

Dining room

Guest suite

after

second floor

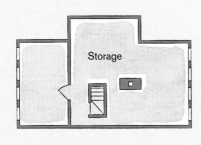

Storage

before

Playroom

Bedroom

Master bedroom

Bunkroom

after

Cottage-style materials in the U-shaped kitchen blend well with the adjacent open rooms. Light maple Shaker cabinets with panel doors were chosen for their simplicity and left natural instead of painted. Laminate countertops have a rolled edge so it looks like it's all one piece. Flooring is original wide red oak boards.

Living spaces are filled with multipaned windows overlooking the backyard and patio, providing good indoor/outdoor connection while visibly extending interior space.

Exterior Facelift

Although the small summer cottage sits among several 3,000- to 5,000-sq.-ft. shingle-sided mini-mansions, it doesn't look totally out of place. Instead, its style meshes neatly with the fabric of Jamestown. People pass by and don't even notice, simply thinking the cottage has been there for years just the way it is now. Finely crafted exterior detailing straight out of a 1900 pattern book gives the cottage a classic look—

Windows high in the family room wall provide privacy from nearby neighbors and don't get in the way of furniture placement.

Know Your House

FROM THE TIME IT WAS BUILT, this little dwelling was a cottage, plain and simple. Preserving that authentic character became priority number one. After gutting the interior, pieces worth reusing were sensitively put back together. Old steam radiators were replumbed, original plumbing fixtures refinished, and even the claw-foot tub was reporcelained. Original wide plank flooring was reused, as were all solid wood doors, including knobs and hinges. Windows were replaced with energy-efficient wood units and detailed with simple square stock surrounds and deep sills. To pay homage to the cottage style, beadboard sheeting was added to a wainscot in the master bath and to the main staircase. Original square sheet board and batten was reproduced on the ceiling, both for its character and inexpensive cost.

The beauty of this transformation is that the entire house is basically new—electrical, plumbing, heating, furnace, hot water system, foundation. Yet, it's still a charming cottage. Nothing is overdone. And it was accomplished for less than $100 a sq. ft.

A simple outdoor shower built to resemble the cottage interior detailing allows family and guests to wash off beach grit and sand before entering the house.

exposed rafter tails feature curved ends; simple wood brackets support the 14-in. roof overhang; and windows have heavy wooden sills.

The renovation is successful because it is timeless, thanks in large part to its appropriate scale and proportion. The scale of the house could have been lost by adding a full second story. With the subtle proportion kept smaller, passersby relate to a single-story home, not a flat two-story box.

Red cedar shingles, traditional in Jamestown, will darken to a grayish brown hue in time, contrasting nicely with the soft white trim. Copper gutters, too, will weather to a soft green patina. Architectural-grade slate gray/green asphalt covers the roof. A rebuilt chimney of old Boston paver brick is topped with a traditional bluestone cap. Familiar exterior details such as these hint at the romance found inside.

The window arrangement in the family room provides space for a hidden interior chaseway on one side housing a metal furnace flue that angles up the cathedral ceiling, then links up with the chimney, built of paver brick.

Finely crafted exterior details give the cottage a classic look— exposed rafter tails with curved ends, and simple wood brackets supporting the roof overhang. Red cedar shingles, traditional in Jamestown, eventually will darken to a grayish brown.

Urban Townhouse Renewal

Julie and Rick Harlan Schneider went against the tide when they bought their Washington, D.C., townhouse. Instead of a big new house with a large yard, they opted for a small 1930s townhouse on a spit of land. Instead of a sprawling, far-flung suburb a long drive from the office, they picked an urban neighborhood that's a short bus or bike ride from work.

The house was only 1,600 sq. ft. and had been neglected for decades. The rooms were dark and dingy, the kitchen and bathroom were dated and intolerably small, the den was murky, and the exterior was a visual hodgepodge. But for Rick, an architect accredited in "green," eco-friendly design, and Julie, an environmental policy professional, the place was perfect.

They had been searching for a house that would support an eco-friendly lifestyle, and this one did so on all fronts.

WISH LIST

Use "green" materials and systems

Retain as much of the original structure as possible

Modernize the house while respecting its history

Redo the kitchen, bathroom, and den

Bring in light and color

as it is today

Painted a lustrous white, the original newel post, balusters, and molding convey the dignity of the 1930s house. The refinished wood floors form a satiny path from the entry through to the den, in an open, contemporary spatial flow.

Situated at the end of the block, the townhouse has yard space on three sides. The long side faces east, flooding the house with morning sun.

It occupied a sunny corner lot in a quiet, leafy neighborhood within walking distance of stores, schools, parks, churches, and the library. It was structurally sound and had a floor plan that worked, making a major overhaul or teardown unnecessary. And beneath the grime and old paint were many distinctive 1930s-era ornamental details.

Rick's firm, Inscape Studio, designed an update that celebrates the vintage character of the house but adds contemporary spirit. The "green" renovation emphasizes energy efficiency, environmental protection, and a healthy living environment. Rick made only essential changes, redoing the kitchen and bathroom and updating the den. New finishes and colors shine up the other rooms.

A shade lighter in color and filled with sunlight, the den visually enlarges the dining room. Windows and a French door still form a traditional wall of glass between the spaces.

as it was ...

Sleek black and chrome den furniture harmonizes with the stainless-steel appliances and charcoal granite kitchen counters, smoothing the connection between the contemporary kitchen and more traditional den. Frosted-glass cabinet doors reflect the light and form of the den windows.

Space, Sun, and Style in the Den and Kitchen

Although the 170-sq.-ft. den was one of the biggest rooms in the house, it was drab, uninviting, and accessible only by tramping through the dining room. Not only that, but the 70-sq.-ft. kitchen—a narrow sliver of a room—bumped up against the den wall. Rick improved both rooms by removing the wall between the den and the kitchen and connecting the spaces with a counter/breakfast table. Together, the kitchen and den form a casual, cheery living area where Rick and Julie come to play with their twin toddlers.

Great Moves

Walls around a bedroom closet cornered the 27-sq.-ft. bathroom against the wall at the end of a narrow passage. By eliminating the closet and hallway, Rick enlarged the bathroom to a comfortable 45 sq. ft. and gave it a more accessible entry from the stair hall. He moved the tub/shower away from the window to an interior wall so that shower water no longer gathers on the sill and can run down inside the wall. Now that the tub has been relocated, sunlight streams into the room, never blocked by the shower curtain. Relocating the tub also made way for a private entry to the master bedroom. When the main door is closed, the room becomes a master bath. The commode stayed in place, which avoided the expense of moving the waste line.

▣ before and after ▣

first floor

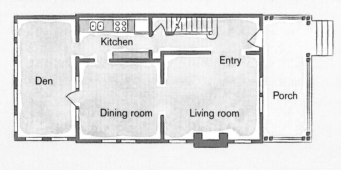

before

after

second floor

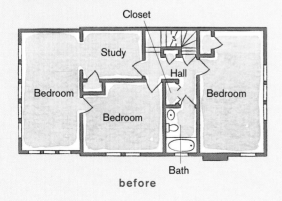

before

after

Surrounded by interior and exterior windows and bathed in airy blue, the den is both a solar room and a sunny gathering place for the family. A retro-style ceiling fan, one of many in the house, keeps the room cool.

New finishes—light-color ceramic floor tile and smooth drywall, painted pale blue—bring light and polish to the den. They also equip the south-facing room as a solar collector. Light from the den's big windows is reflected into interior rooms, and the floor tiles, together with the original concrete slab beneath them, absorb solar heat to help warm the house in winter.

Melding Vintage and Contemporary

Simplicity of design and sympathetic details artfully knit old and new. The remodeled kitchen is sleek and contemporary, while expressing an industrial "1930s modern" aesthetic that respects the house's roots. Birchwood and frosted-glass cabinet doors have flat fronts and finger pulls rather than handles. The appliances are brushed stainless steel. Rick planned to tile the floor, but when he pulled up the worn vinyl, he uncovered original oak, which was dusty but sound. Delighted, he resealed it to match the other gleaming wood floors in the house.

The marriage of traditional and modern is celebrated in room connections. Traditional trim frames the openings, clearly marking transitions between living room, dining room, and den, even as light from the den fuses the three spaces. Sophisticated colors give each room a distinct atmosphere and combine to make a fresh, vibrant interior.

The handsome old newel post and balusters lend grace to the house. Rick retained these and other original trim features, highlighting them with white paint.

In the revamped bathroom, Rick installed wainscoting and tile flooring. It's traditional in style but sings the same tune as the modern yet evocative frameless mirror, chrome light fixture, and sleek pedestal sink.

For aesthetic as well as environmental reasons, Rick and Julie reused original features throughout the house. Cleaned and repainted, the old doors and windows, wide moldings and deep baseboards, handsome newel posts and tailored balusters add luster and period personality. A coat of ivory paint brings out the stylish geometry of the masonry fireplace.

Rick did design one new feature: radiator covers to hide the ugly pipes. But the streamlined boxes, used upstairs and downstairs, lend

Rick designed contemporary radiator covers that fit in without calling attention to themselves. Basic boxes with perforated metal faces, they are painted to match the walls and trim.

consistency and do not compete with the more decorative period details. Original casing around doorways makes a classy border marker between spaces, cleanly separating rooms that are connected visually but differ in ambiance. An array of sophisticated, complementary colors allows diversity from room to room but paints a dynamic overall picture.

Where New Meets Old

New meets old in the Schneiders' house like a young man and his grandfather: They clearly are different, but they get along well because they are family. It's easy to tell when you are in an original or new part of the house, but the rooms harmonize well. The new spaces draw traditional elements from the original house, and the old rooms have been invigorated with complementary, contemporary details. The redone kitchen, for example, is sleek and streamlined, yet its oak floors are original to the house and the brushed stainless appliances, frosted-glass cabinet doors, and smooth birch cabinetry evoke the 1930s vision of "modern." In the bathroom, Rick mixed a contemporary pedestal sink with wainscoting and floor tile reminiscent of the '30s. The old living room retains the original trim but glows with a rich new red wall color. New radiator boxes are simple and contemporary in shape, but painted to meld with the walls and molding.

All of the original molding and five-panel wood doors, complete with original hardware, remain; polished up, they enrich the upstairs space. Glazed transoms bring sunlight into the hallway; they can be adjusted to control airflow.

Green Systems and Design

As environmentalists, Rick and Julie rely on nature more than machines to keep their house comfortable in temperature and filled with light. They installed air-conditioning but only on the second floor. They use it only in the hottest weather and mostly at night. Closing the bedroom doors keeps the cooled air upstairs for comfortable sleeping; if the first floor needs cooling, the doors are opened and the upstairs ceiling fans are turned on.

Closing the louvered shutters and Venetian blinds, opening the windows, and running the ceiling fans keep the house cool the rest of the time. Rick restored the old transom windows, which had been painted shut. Now they not only channel sunlight into interior

French doors to the back bedroom and transoms elsewhere diffuse the upstairs spaces with natural light. Soft, natural wall colors harmonize with the wood floors and white trim.

rooms but also enhance airflow. In winter, sun pours through uncovered and gauzily curtained windows to brighten and warm the house. Passive solar heat released from the den augments the work of the gas furnace.

Rick strategically chose a French gray tone to coat the exterior of the house. Ultraviolet rays bounce off the light-colored surface so that the house does not absorb and emit excess heat, becoming an environmentally detrimental "heat island." Using a single color made aesthetic sense, too. It tamed the jumble of brick, stucco, Tudoresque timbers, and wood framing, giving the house a clean, unified look.

For Rick and Julie, the living space of the house is not confined within four walls. They spend a lot of time on their front porch. With a ceiling fan that matches those inside, it's a comfortable three-season room. On many a balmy evening, the family goes out to the porch to have dinner. They can dine alfresco, while greeting their neighborhood friends and savoring the feeling of community.

Light gray paint unifies the exterior, covering a conglomeration of materials and reflecting UV rays away. Black bands and white trim highlight the windows, and the porch stands out in crisp white.

THE SEVEN

Know Your Palette

RICK AND JULIE wanted their house to be environmentally sensitive in materials as well as design. They carefully selected products that are safe for the environment and make a house healthy to live in. The paints and floor sealants have low amounts of polluting VOCS (volatile organic compounds). The light color roofing and exterior paint reflect ultraviolet rays, keeping the house from heating up and raising the temperature of its surroundings.

All the appliances are energy-efficient models. Lighting is fluorescent, to save energy. The showerhead is low-flow. The furnace burns natural gas. Passive solar heat, absorbed by concrete under the den's tile floor, also helps heat the house. Ceiling fans do much of the cooling.

The kitchen cabinets are made from formaldehyde-free, sustainable harvested wood, and were shipped flat to save energy in transportation. The cabinets they replaced are not moldering in a landfill; Rick is using them in the mother-in-law apartment he's remodeling in the English basement apartment.

Design with a Difference

Additions don't have to blend with a house to belong. Nor do they have to be big to make a big improvement. Jeff Wheeler and Wendy Williams added just 150 sq. ft. to the back of their Minneapolis foursquare but, like a brilliant actor with a bit part, the avant-garde little bumpout steals the show.

Jeff had lived in the 1923 stucco house for several years before meeting Wendy. The dark, squared-off rooms were adequate for him, if boring. After they married and had two children, Jeff and Wendy were determined to change the house in a way that would make it theirs as a family. The plan: to convert the kitchen into a larger and more versatile kitchen-family area.

Tacking on a one-story stucco look-alike never crossed their minds. As creative people—Jeff's a photojournalist and Wendy a professional musician—they wanted the addition to make a bold, creative statement. Since it would be on the

WISH LIST

Provide a versatile, family-friendly living space

Fill the kitchen with natural light

Add storage—lots of it and a wide variety

Improve views and access to the backyard

The homeowners particularly like the sociable character of the addition at night. An entry light beams a welcome against the ribbed steel walls, and the interior glows through big, friendly windows.

The house still looks staid and traditional on the public, or front, side. Only in back, out of sight from the street, does it break loose with a fun add-on.

back of the house and hidden from general view, they felt free to charge it with personality. They asked architect Geoffrey Warner to replace a tiny porch and deck with a new deck and an open, light-filled space containing a breakfast nook, plentiful storage, and a mudroom area. Warner created a curving, metal kitchen extension and scooped out the existing kitchen, fusing it with the standout addition to form a contemporary 350-sq.-ft. space that dazzles both inside and out.

Mixing Modern and Traditional on the Outside

The exterior of the addition contrasts with the existing house in almost every way. Rather than genteel stucco, it is clad in industrial metal—copper sheeting with a band of shiny galvanized steel flashing, and a jutting, corrugated steel entryway. Instead of a conventional, pitched roof, the addition has a curved profile and a flat top over the entry. The windows are trimless and single-paned, unlike the shuttered double-hung units on the front of the house. The entire structure bursts out at a cockeyed angle, defiantly breaking the grid of the foursquare building. The irregular shape of the deck and the offbeat position of the two deck stairways—one spilling into the yard and the other running to the driveway—accentuate the odd geometry.

Yet the mix works. Why? Because Warner applied an artist's eye to the use of simple honest materials and forms. The design, though modern, is restrained. Essentially, the addition is made of only three materials—metal, glass, and wood—all unornamented and striking in their own right. And the building's shapes and angles are sculptural but essential, expressing the function of the space.

The arched roof, for instance, lends light and airiness to the interior while skirting the stairway windows on the existing house. Corrugated-steel panels mounted on steel posts form a starkly beautiful composition that shields the entryway. Attaching the addition

The industrial materials, rounded roof, and skewed angle of the addition defy the conventions of the 1923 foursquare. The addition is not totally rebellious, though; like the old house it has stepped windows, horizontal rooflines, and a mix of light and dark.

The planes of copper walls and corrugated steel, punctuated by exposed metal fasteners, take on a sculptural quality. To prevent a chemical reaction between the copper and steel, they are separated by a seam filled with rubberized flashing.

Warner dissolved the visual barrier between indoors and out by running a countertop across the divide. The metal table in the covered entryway seems to slice through the wall and merge with the shoe wall inside the building.

Great Moves

Even though the addition is small, the kitchen almost doubled in size. Rather than add an entire room, Warner combined old and new spaces, recasting the existing 200-sq.-ft. kitchen as the food preparation area and putting the breakfast area and entry vestibule in the 150-sq.-ft. add-on.

Attaching the addition at an angle helps delineate areas within the integrated space. The 6-ft. end of the addition forms an inviting enclosure for the breakfast table, while the 11-ft. end provides ample wall space for cabinets.

■ before and after ■

first floor

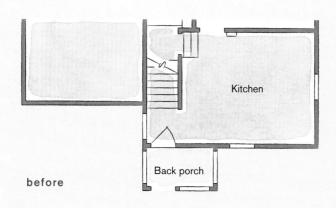

Kitchen

Back porch

before

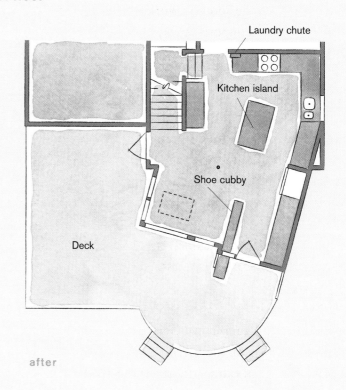

Laundry chute

Kitchen island

Shoe cubby

Deck

after

Know Your Passions

WENDY AND JEFF WANTED the addition to be creative, adventurous, and playful, just as they need to be in their work as musician and photographer. The lighthearted shapes and daring materials are a continual source of delight and rediscovery for them.

The structure is even more fun and personal because it is rife with subtle allusions to photography and music, the things that Wendy and Jeff love. The arch-topped, copper-skinned addition looks a little like a music box, just as the angled addition recalls the shape of a piano. The entry bumpout, sheathed in horizontally ribbed, corrugated steel, suggests a lens zooming out from a camera.

The shiny metal light fixtures inside the kitchen are reminiscent of photographer's lights, and the Fireslate counters look like tabletops in a photography lab. For architect Geoffrey Warner, the bare steel supporting post and beam have the innate beauty of an old camera tripod.

at an angle gives it optimal positioning as well as creative energy: The big windows face the yard rather than the unsightly garage, and the deck reaches toward the driveway, providing convenient access.

Another reason the addition works is that it is compatible with the existing house in important ways. Color is one unifying element. The corrugated steel harmonizes in tone with the stucco, and dark copper siding caps the steel in the same way that dark asphalt roofing caps the stucco. Geometry is used for harmony as well as contrast. The flat roof of the entry and the horizontal bands at each end of the addition's curved roof correspond to the eave lines of the main house. The side of the addition aligns roughly with a nearby window on the existing house. Just as windows step up the wall of the house, the windows on the addition step up too. Distinction in scale also helps keep the peace between the spirited addition and the staid main house. The addition is small enough that its energy and excitement make the house more interesting, without overpowering it.

Organized but Flexible on the Inside

Shapes and angles organize the open interior into linked sections for maximum flexibility. An island with seating space and an electrical hookup doubles as an extra work surface in the roomy L-shaped food preparation area. A long wall of birch cabinets angles all the way from

There is no view on the north side of the addition, so Warner used the space for cabinets. Outside, it presents a solid, private wall to the neighbors, with slim, high windows to admit light. The deck intersects the addition at an artful angle and echoes the arc of the vaulted roof.

Where New Meets Old

Warner used contrast between new and old not only to distinguish the kitchen from the main house, but also to energize the room itself.

Old and new parts of the kitchen are distinct, but resonate with each other through compatible details. the angled walls and barrel-vaulted ceiling announce the addition by taking off where new joins old. Likewise, the maple strip flooring in the addition runs perpendicular to the old. The walls of the addition, terracotta in color, form a vivid contrast with the yellow backsplash in the food prep area.

But threads of continuity bind the spaces together. The ceilings are white and the floor tones blend. Birch cabinetry, charcoal black countertops, and light wood trim are used consistently. Above the sink, one window remains wrapped in the original dark woodwork, looking like a postcard sent from the old house.

The top of the shoe wall continues the line of the entryway shelf, even folding over the end the same way. Both surfaces are metal; the outdoor one is weather-resistant, painted galvanized steel and the indoor one is dark, hot-rolled steel that matches the Fireslate counters.

the kitchen proper to the back door. At the kitchen end, the cabinets store china and appliances; at the other end, they morph into a broom closet and a place for coats, hats, and gloves. Across from the coat closet, a wooden partition with a black metal countertop (hot rolled steel with a paste wax finish) defines a mudroom zone. The partition houses shelves as well as a grid of cubbies that Jeff and Wendy specially requested for stashing all the shoes that pile up by the door.

The back of the "shoe wall" shapes a cozy enclosure for the breakfast nook. An austere, black-steel post and beam occupy the spot where the kitchen wall once stood, marking another boundary of the breakfast corner while keeping the area open to the friendly kitchen.

Warner slipped a message center into a low-ceilinged area by the stairs. A simple wood table and a black, wall-mounted magnet board connect this area aesthetically to the kitchen, with its palette

The mix of light wood floors and cabinets, dark countertops, and metal accents is clean and classy—and it was not expensive to achieve. All the cabinets, including the metal-framed frosted-glass models, are standard items. Fireslate, the countertop material, is half the price of granite.

of light wood and dark metal surfaces, and draw the space into active use.

Natural light suffuses the kitchen. Warner wrapped the breakfast area with large windows and, for good measure, inserted a skylight in the airy, barrel-vaulted ceiling. Clerestory windows along the cabinet wall soak in the sun without absorbing storage space. Two glass doors, one at the mudroom and one by the back stairs, act as full-height windows, and open the room to the deck and the outdoors.

The abundance of light makes a warm, cheerful place for the family to hang out. Jeff and Wendy use it as a breakfast room and sunny sitting area, as they anticipated they would. With two toddlers, they've discovered that it is also a great playroom. The open spaces and bright colors make a natural environment for kids. When their daughter first learned to walk, she happily made laps around the island. Some of the cookbook shelves on the ends of the island have been taken over temporarily by toys and a play kitchen.

By now Jeff and Wendy know their party guests will end up in the kitchen too. No problem: The island and the breakfast table are on casters, so it's a snap to move them around to set up a buffet or clear the way for a crowd.

as it was ...

Architects and Designers

Ransom Baldasare
Webber & Studio, Inc.
300 West Avenue, Suite 1322
Austin, TX 78701
(512) 236-1032
www.webberhanzlik.com
pp. 24–35

Jonathan Barnes, AIA, NCARB
Jonathan Barnes Architecture and Design
153 East Main Street, Suite 300
Columbus, OH 43215
(614) 228-7311
www.jbadusa.com
pp. 82–91

Carol Beth Cozen, AIA,
Demery Matthews, Henry Wong
Cozen Architecture
1635 19th Street
Manhattan Beach, CA 90266
(310) 802-0403
www.cozenarchitecture.com
pp. 100–111

Ralph Cunningham, AIA
Cunningham+Quill Architects
1054 31st Street NW
Washington, D.C. 20007
(202) 337-0090
www.cunninghamquill.com
pp. 14–23

Ron DiMauro, AIA
Ronald F. DiMauro Architects
28 Bellevue Avenue
Newport, RI 02840
(401) 846-6868
pp. 158–167

Jeremiah Eck, FAIA
Jeremiah Eck Architects
560 Harrison Avenue, Suite 403
Boston, MA 02118
(617) 367-9696
www.jearch.com
pp. 142–151

Robert Gerloff, AIA
Robert Gerloff Residential Architects
4007 Sheridan Avenue South
Minneapolis, MN 55410
(612) 927-5913
www.residentialarchitects.com
pp. 76–81
pp. 152–157

Mark Larson, AIA
Susan Nackers Ludwig
Rehkamp Larson Architects, Inc.
2732 West 43rd Street
Minneapolis, MN 55410
(612) 285-7275
www.rehkamplarson.com
pp. 36–45

Robert Mahrer
202 Frederick Street
Santa Cruz, CA 95062
(831) 462-9062
pp. 56–63

Jim Samsel, AIA
Samsel Architects
60 Biltmore Avenue,
Asheville, NC 28801
(828) 253-1124
www.samselarchitects.com
pp. 112–121

Rick Harlan Schneider, AIA, LEED
Inscape Studio
1215 Connecticut Avenue NW, Third Floor
Washington, D.C. 20036
(202) 416-0333
www.inscapestudio.com
pp. 168–177

Matthew Schoenherr, AIA
Z:Architecture
1052 Main Street
Branford, CT 06405
(203)-488-8484
pp. 2–13
pp. 92–99

Pi Smith, AIA
Smith and Vansant Architects
15 River Road
Norwich, VT 05055
(802) 649-5515
www.smithandvansant.com
pp. 64–75

Mark Stein
Stein/Troost Architects
One Morgan Avenue
Norwalk, CT 06851
(203) 831-9983
pp. 46–55

Geoffrey Warner
Brandon Sigrist
Warner + Asmus Architects
550 Vandalia Street #314
St. Paul, MN 55114
(651) 647-6650
www.warnerasmus.com
pp. 178–185

Mark Wilson, Architect
Boccardo Roberts Architecture & Design
1 San Carlos Avenue
Sausalito, CA 94965
(415) 331-0606
pp. 122–131

Mitch Yockey, AIA
Boxwood
1218 Third Avenue, Suite 1412
Seattle, WA 98101
(206) 343-0236
www.eboxwood.com
pp. 132–141